Praise for *Passionate Leadership*

"I always say that being positive doesn't just make you better; it makes everyone around you better. That's leadership. These guys connect positivity with hard work and a willingness to grow in an effective way. Teachers, principals, business leaders, coaches, and anyone who leads a team can benefit from their message."

—Jon Gordon
Best-selling author of *The Energy Bus* and *The Power of Positive Leadership*

"Move over excuses, there is no room for you here. *Passionate Leadership* will have you looking inward and asking yourself the tough questions to upgrade your impact. This book supports what top performers have understood for ages—all leadership begins with self-leadership."

—Daniel Bauer
Author of *The Better Leaders Better Schools Roadmap*

"If you are a school leader looking to reignite your passion for the work you do each and every day for your students and staff, then get ready for *Passionate Leadership; Creating a Culture of Success in Every School*. Authors Salome Thomas-EL, Joseph Jones, and T.J. Vari have teamed up to share their formula for cultivating a vibrant culture by helping you uncover what they call 'Trip Traps' and developed an actionable blueprint to help you find your passion again. Each chapter contains practical tips from leaders in the field along with reflective questions to help you focus on the important work you do."

—Jimmy Casas
Educator, speaker, leadership coach, and author of *Culturize*

"In my travels to schools around the world, there is no doubt in my mind that the most successful teachers and principals succeed *because* they are passionate about their students and communities. In *Passionate Leadership*, the authors empower readers with fresh ways to recapture their passion, build strong school cultures, and embrace the power of positive celebrations. This is a must read for every educator."

—Manny Scott
Best-selling author, speaker, and servant leader

"*Passionate Leadership* shows us how classroom, school, and district leaders can tap into their passions and evolve as educators, all in the name of promoting the success of students. The blueprint to success in the educational world can be found in this inspirational book."

—Brad Currie
NASSP National Assistant Principal of the Year and #Satchat co-creator

"*Passionate Leadership* is the book every school leader should be sure to get their hands on to spread the hunger for learning throughout their school communities. This book is full of ideas from experienced leaders who share how they support their school cultures and help even the most struggling educators thrive and succeed."

—Shelly Sanchez Terrell
Digital innovator, author, and teacher

"*Passionate Leadership* is the spark that will ignite your flame for the work you do and turn it into a fire! Salome, Joseph and T.J. provide practical resources, examples and actionable steps you can use tomorrow. Wherever you are in the journey, *Passionate Leadership* will provide a light to lead the way."

—Jessica Cabeen
Nationally Distinguished Principal, author, and speaker

"*Passionate Leadership: Creating a Culture of Success in Every School* is a book that will inspire, energize, and rejuvenate educators serving in any teaching and leadership role. It will both challenge you to become even better while also validating all the good you are currently doing. It is a book written by practitioners with documented track records of success. The stories, ideas, tips, and strategies contained within this book serve as a road map for continuous improvement and creating a culture in which all stakeholders invest in each other—most importantly, the students they serve. I wholeheartedly recommend this book for passionate educators everywhere who truly wish to make a difference in our profession."

—Jeffrey Zoul, EdD
Author, speaker, leadership coach, and President of ConnectEDD

"This is an uplifting, practical, and inspirational guide for leaders, regardless your title! It gives insights and guidance for new leaders and new fuel for the experienced educators. The real vignettes from current leaders remind us of the importance of our work and gives us all something to build upon! Great messages all around, from the heart of leaders, to the heart of leaders."

—Derek McCoy
Middle school principal, author, and 2014
National Digital Principal of the Year

"Masterfully written and destined to ignite systemic change. *Passionate Leadership* includes some of the best vignettes from the field I've ever read. This book is a blueprint for creating the conditions required to learn. The authors thoughtfully address all the moving parts of passionate leadership using technical tips and clear take-aways to inspire change. *Passionate Leadership* is the perfect blend of research and inspiration."

—Brad Gustafson
Award-winning principal, author, and speaker

"*Passionate Leadership: Creating a Culture of Success in Every School* is a call-to-action that will inspire every leader to rekindle, grow, and sustain their passion for education. Jones, Thomas-EL, and Vari share stories, research, and examples that will compel you to act in powerful ways to serve your school community and to overcome obstacles. Schools are meant to be environments that spark abundant passion; fueling a culture that ignites the desire to be a lifelong learner, resulting in growth. We want our schools to foster a learning culture where every individual is wholeheartedly committed to advancing, and this book will support you in your journey. Filled with actionable ideas, *Passionate Leadership* is one you'll return to in your pursuit to continuously improve, while simultaneously transforming lives."

—Elisabeth Bostwick
Instructional coach, speaker, and Author of
Take the L.E.A.P.: Ignite a Culture of Innovation

"As I visit hundreds of schools and districts across the U.S. and Canada every year, I share my passion for kids and respect anyone who has that same passion! This book is a great manual for those who want to reignite their passion for this work!"

—Robert Jackson
National education consultant, author, and former NFL player

"If you're looking to make meaningful and lasting changes in your classroom, school building or district, *Passionate Leadership* is the right book for you. The authors Jones, Thomas-EL, and Vari address possible pitfalls and how to avoid them. With all the great leadership books available, leaders should choose *Passionate Leadership* because it will inspire action from reflection to make real change."

—Starr Sackstein
Author, speaker, and humanities lead learner
West Hempstead Union Free Schools

"Education is the engine of a great society and effective leadership is the fuel! This book conceptualizes leadership passion in a way that is accessible to anyone with the desire to lead a school to greatness. The framework provided in this book is sound, practical, and relevant to school leaders at all levels. This book is a must read for those genuinely concerned about improving school effectiveness."

—Anthony Muhammad, PhD
Author and educational consultant

"As a district leader, principal, and instructional coach, I have always been passionate about my work with and for educators and students. The work for children and the battles that administrators and educators face at the frontline are so important that we need to continue to ignite our passion for building positive school cultures. In *Passionate Leadership*, the authors do a great job of inspiring us all to reflect on the impact we make on our students and schools each day. If you want to become a better educator or leader for your students, you must read this book!"

—Dr. Rosa Isiah
Director of Elementary and Instructional Supports,
Norwalk La Mirada USD

"Through research, real examples, and powerful reflection Salome Thomas-EL, Joseph Jones, and T.J. Vari have created an invaluable road map for leaders to better serve the children that are entrusted in our care each day. The authors help us to recognize the common obstacles that get in the way of high levels of learning and instead build bridges to success for ALL students. Through the pages of *Passionate Leadership: Creating a Culture of Success in Every School* you will find inspiration, motivation, and a drive to be the best leader that you can be. It is a resource I wish I had as I started my leadership journey and I highly recommend it to all educators."

—Beth Houf
Principal, Fulton Middle School, Co-author of *Lead Like a PIRATE:
Make School Amazing for Students and Staff*

"Education leaders, listen up! Whatever book you're reading right now, put it down, and pick this book up right away. This book is not just for principals or administrators—it's for any passionate person who works with and leads students. We are ALL leaders. As the 2019 North Dakota Teacher of the Year and advocate for kids everywhere, I cannot give *Passionate Leadership: Creating a Culture of Success in Every School* high enough praise. This book will hook you from the very first page, as it includes passionate real-life scenarios from leaders still in schools, immediate takeaways to use in your schools tomorrow, and tools to reshape your thinking. It's one of those books you will highlight, underline, fill with sticky-notes, and come back to time and time again.

Teaching and leading are far from easy, and this book is just the positive pick-me-up you need to reignite or reaffirm the passion burning within you."

—Kayla Delzer
2019 North Dakota Teacher of the Year, Globally
awarded educator, author, CEO: Top Dog Teaching, Inc.

"*Passionate Leadership* provides a road map for educators and leaders who want to build positive and caring cultures in their schools! My entire career as a teacher and principal has been fueled by my passion for kids and our staff! The authors have put into words not only a pathway for a mindset shift, they light the fire to help you get it DONE! This book will give every reader the inspiration to reignite their passion for years to come!"

—Amber Teamann
Award-winning principal, Whitt Elementary, Wylie ISD, Texas

"Passion is about vision and the guiding principles that fuel our work with teachers, students, and families. It is also about the energy, excitement, and enthusiasm that we demonstrate in our daily work, which inspires others to join and identify with our vision. Rarely is someone inspired by a leader who lacks passion for their work. School improvement is not easy, but when we bring our passion for change and growth, we can overcome even the most difficult circumstances. If we are going to build the capacity to do the work that needs to be done in every school, we must ignite a coalition to support students and families in new and different ways. *Passionate Leadership* provides the formula for all of us to create the commitment we need to work together, collectively, for the success that we all know is possible within our current educational systems around the world."

—Dr. Jacquelyn O. Wilson
Director of the Delaware Academy for School
Leadership at the University of Delaware

"Student learning is a relationship between teachers and learners. In order to foster and grow such learning environments, strong leadership is required. We can no longer operate in transactional spaces that promote silos. Schools are dynamic ecosystems that require transformational, visionary leadership, that is student centered. *Passionate Leadership* unpacks the complexity of school leadership in an effort to build communities where students, educators, families, and other stakeholders experience success!"

—Dorrell Green
Superintendent, Red Clay Consolidated School District

"My entire career as a teacher, school and district leader has been fueled by my passion for our students and schools. My goal has always been to build positive classroom and school cultures that inspire others to care about our profession. Culture is built and cultivated by gaining trust of and building relationships with stakeholders. While positive culture is a feeling you get when walking into a school or classroom, it is intentionally built and grown. In *Passionate Leadership*, Thomas-EL, Jones, and Vari have written the manual on how we can commit to serving our students and communities in a powerful way. After you read this book, you will feel a spark igniting you to be even more passionate about our kids and their success."

—Jenny Nauman
National Distinguished Principal and Assistant
Superintendent, Cape Henlopen School District

"In an era of high stakes testing and accountability as the key measures of school and student success, the authors provide a powerful blueprint for leaders to rethink what's important in our schools. *Passionate Leadership* offers practical strategies, real stories and "how to" guidance that will inspire every educator to do great things for all students.

After more than forty-five years in education, I know firsthand about the power of creating a positive and supportive culture with passionate educators and engaged students. The authors have found a solutions-oriented formula that makes schools inviting learning environments students and teachers deserve. *Passionate Leadership* is a must read!"

—Steven H. Godowsky, EdD
Retired superintendent and former Delaware Secretary of Education

"All school communities need passionate leaders who are committed to meeting the needs of ALL students! Such leaders must be committed, inquisitive, and reflection and action oriented. They must desire to grow and improve. This book takes that into account as it pushes the reader to consider how they think about their leadership, their ability to motivate themselves and others, and the steps and actions needed to be the leader others desire to follow and support. The takeaways and tips are invaluable as they provide direct instruction through the stories of other strong and successful leaders. If one wishes to be a relationship-builder who moves the needle through passion and influence rather than title and authority, this is indeed a worthwhile read!"

—Mark Holodick, EdD
Superintendent, Brandywine School District

"Three exceptional administrators shed new light on why passion is so important in education. The vivid stories in this timely book go beyond exhortations to show in detail how inspired leaders transform schools, empower teachers, and enrich students."

—Robert L. Hampel
School of Education, University of Delaware,
Author of *Fast and Curious: A History of Shortcuts in American Education* (2017)

"As the Delaware State Teacher of the Year, I traveled around to a number of schools and heard from teachers and leaders from across the country. It was evident to me at the time that the real difference maker for what distinguishes a great teacher or a great school can be summed up in one word: *passion*. In reading *Passionate Leadership*, I was simply reminded that we must come together with a growth mindset, more will than ever, and the celebratory attitude that our schools need for us to be our best every single day. Don't read this book once or twice, read it once or twice every year."

—Dr. Lea Wainwright
French Teacher and 2014 Delaware State Teacher of the Year

"Education is the most critical aspect of our society. Principals and schools have the responsibility to educate children to be thoughtful and enterprising citizens for the greater good of the world in which we live. All students can learn in an environment that is caring with adults who nurture the "whole" student, including mind, body, and spirit. A principal's task is to create that environment by developing a vision and strategically cultivating other leaders in the school to stand behind it. Great principals recognize that everyone in the school must be held accountable for real success to become a reality. Leadership is a shared responsibility, and it's only passionate leaders who inspire others to greatness by *being* the change that we wish to see in the world. As the principal of the Early College High School at Delaware State University, my mission is to prepare students to do college-level work by the time they are 15 years old. That simply cannot happen without passion. This book, *Passionate Leadership*, offers a how-to manual on having passion in whatever area you're leading. Read it, and you'll be ready to take your school to the next level."

—Dr. Evelyn Edney
Principal, Early College High School at Delaware State University

Passionate Leadership

Creating a Culture of Success in Every School

Salome Thomas-EL

Joseph Jones

T.J. Vari

Foreword by Todd Whitaker

FOR INFORMATION:

Corwin

A SAGE Company

2455 Teller Road

Thousand Oaks, California 91320

(800) 233-9936

www.corwin.com

SAGE Publications Ltd.

1 Oliver's Yard

55 City Road

London EC1Y 1SP

United Kingdom

SAGE Publications India Pvt. Ltd.

B 1/I 1 Mohan Cooperative Industrial Area

Mathura Road, New Delhi 110 044

India

SAGE Publications Asia-Pacific Pte. Ltd.

18 Cross Street #10-10/11/12

China Square Central

Singapore 048423

Publisher: Arnis Burvikovs

Development Editor: Desirée A. Bartlett

Senior Editorial Assistant: Eliza B. Erickson

Production Editor: Amy Schroller

Copy Editor: Diane DiMura

Typesetter: C&M Digitals (P) Ltd.

Proofreader: Laura Webb

Indexer: Sheila Bodell

Cover Designer: Dally Verghese

Marketing Manager: Sharon Pendergast

Library of Congress Cataloging-in-Publication Data

Names: Thomas-EL, Salome, author. | Jones, Joseph, author. | Vari, T. (T.J.), author.

Title: Passionate leadership : creating a culture of success in any school / Salome Thomas-EL, Head of School, Thomas Edison Charter School, Joseph Jones, Director of Assessment and Accountability at New Castle County Vocational, Technical School District, T.J. Vari - Assistant Superintendent, Appoquinimink School District.

Description: Thousand Oaks, California : Corwin, [2018] | Includes bibliographical references and index.

Identifiers: LCCN 2019006736 | ISBN 9781544345697 (pbk. : alk. paper)

Subjects: LCSH: Educational leadership—United States. | School management and organization—United States. | School environment—United States.

Classification: LCC LB2805 .T495 2018 | DDC 371.2—dc23 LC record available at https://lccn.loc.gov/2019006736

Certified Chain of Custody

SUSTAINABLE FORESTRY INITIATIVE

Promoting Sustainable Forestry

www.sfiprogram.org

SFI-01268

SFI label applies to text stock

19 20 21 22 23 10 9 8 7 6 5 4 3 2 1

Contents

Foreword

Passionate teachers and leaders build powerful relationships with students and all members of the school community. They are positive influences on others, have a strong work ethic, and possess a tremendous desire to grow, but educators across the board know that as time goes, the details and hardships of day-to-day work can cause some of us to lose sight of our passion. In *Passionate Leadership*, Salome, Joe, and T.J. have written the manual for educators who are seeking to reignite their passion. This book is written for school leaders who want to build cultures of love, support, care, and high expectations.

Through working with schools and districts across America, I have the opportunity to see how the hard-fought efforts of effective teachers and principals accomplish good across the community. This success does not occur without effective teachers and principals fighting for better outcomes in their schools. My many years of research and teaching educational leadership have allowed me to uncover and enumerate what it means to be excellent in our work in classrooms and beyond. I can say without hesitation that T.J., Joe, and Salome have added a much-needed ingredient to what the best leaders know our schools need to be successful: *passion*. It is clear that one thing great teachers and principals do that others do not is bring passionate leadership into their classrooms, schools, and districts every day.

During my career, I've written many books and have spoken to hundreds if not thousands of groups about what motivates staff members, teachers, and principals during difficult times. One area that is essential is enhancing staff morale through the building of positive school cultures. In many ways, the culture of our schools must be one of care. This can be accomplished through positive communication and openness to change and transformation so that all students are succeeding. Now is the time to build better cultures in our schools so that our teachers and principals have the energy they need to be passionate and excellent, and where our students have the support they need to be successful.

In *Passionate Leadership*, Salome, Joe, and T.J. present the blueprint for what your school and district need to develop and sustain a culture of success. Every teacher and school leader who cares about self-reflection, treating others with respect, and becoming a positive force in their school should read this book. Whether you're looking for technical expertise or inspiration, this book is packed with the power of passion and positivity along with what that can mean for *every* school.

Readers will love the way this book is set up. The formula for passion is simple: 1. We all must desire to grow a culture with deep relationships, 2. Everyone must contribute with no idle onlookers allowed, and 3. Positivity must be the core of our daily work. The book has three sections, with each section dedicated to a different part of the formula, and each individual section has three components as well: The first is comprised of real stories which the authors collected from educators who are in the trenches daily, the second derives from the research that identifies what schools need now, and the third contains technical tips that are provided for implementation as soon as you finish the book.

Whether you're a passionate educator or one who has somehow lost your source of passion, this book can help you move forward on your journey. If you have a desire to grow through feedback, if you want to impact others in your school, or if you simply want to find a way to surround yourself with positive people, this book is an excellent tool. Working to build a culture where passion is sustainable throughout your school is a daunting task, but valuable resources like *Passionate Leadership* make the process easy to understand. The authors are leadership practitioners and champions for all educators, so they know through experience, that the content in this book is genuine.

Lastly, let me say that I was personally inspired by the stories you'll find within the pages of this book. I'm energized by the work that is being done day-in and day-out by passionate teachers and leaders across the nation and around the world, and I hope you'll join me, along with Joe, Salome, and T.J., in developing passionate leadership in every school. Enjoy this groundbreaking book, and you'll be among the many who have become a part of the revolution to improve and innovate what we do in education. *Passionate Leadership* isn't just recommended reading for all school personnel, it should be expected reading for all educators for the important work they do in our schools. Enjoy.

—Todd Whitaker

Professor of Educational Leadership at the University of Missouri
Professor Emeritus at Indiana State University
Author of over 50 books, including
What Great Teachers Do Differently and
What Great Principals Do Differently

Preface

This book is about passionate leadership. At its core, it is a leadership book for people who want to learn more about leading schools, school culture, and igniting a system for passionate people to lead better for the sake of our students. This book offers a formula for bringing passion to the forefront of our work in schools. Herein you will find mantras to live by, inspirational stories from real leaders in the field, reflection questions, visuals and models, takeaways and how-to guidance, along with much more to shape and reshape your thinking, planning, and action regarding your personal passion and the passion that you can fuel for others. Our true desire is that this book is a spark that inspires you to take immediate action.

We wrote this book because we've seen firsthand how the system can beat people down, creating despair and defeat. We've heard from countless people that their morale is low, draining the energy and enthusiasm that they once had and that kids need and deserve. The truth is, it doesn't have to be that way and it doesn't have to be your reality. We've heard from educators who are at the top of their game, making a real difference and inspiring those around them to do the same. We've heard from passionate leaders around the world who can't wait to get up every morning because of their intense drive and the team of people they have with them to achieve success. We gathered their stories, curated the themes that we heard over and over, and synthesized them for our readers. We know that there are educators out there who need a nudge, a simple recharge, people who can lead us into the future but need some support to get there. There are others who have the formula, or parts of it, in place right now, ready to be replicated across the system. This book brings all of the moving parts of passionate leadership together as an understandable and actionable blueprint for every school. We hope you enjoy it.

FEATURES TO GUIDE YOU

Passionate Leadership is designed to guide your thinking, your planning, and your actions. In the Introduction, you will find our first feature called **Trip Traps**. These are the common causes for missing or declining passion. Trip Traps are the reasons why passion is often stifled in schools and why leaders feel that they can't move forward. The good news is that these traps are not insurmountable, and we're going to show you how to avoid falling into them. Additionally within the Introduction, you'll find our **Mantras To Live By.** These are three clear statements that leaders use as self-talk for a *passionate start* to every single day and a *passion pause* for whenever things seem to be going the wrong way. The most passionate leaders who we listened to for the creation of this book had clear and discerning ways that they spoke to themselves and others about growth, core values, work ethic, and positivity. These mantras are meant to be used as an internal self-guiding force and shared with others as regular reminders.

This book is divided into three parts whereby each one uncovers a unique aspect of passionate leadership. All three parts focus on culture and precisely what drives passion in schools from the inside out. Each part opens with an **inspirational story** about a real scenario with real people who made a difference in the lives of young people. This book is written by practitioners for practitioners with examples from the field.

Chapters 1, 3, and 5 provide a framework to get you thinking about specific ideas and inspire you to take action. Each chapter includes a chart to compare a passionate culture to one lacking in passion. The charts compare a learning culture with a teaching culture, a communal culture with an isolated culture, and a celebrated team versus an ignored and admonished one. These three chapters (1, 3, and 5) also demonstrate how a passionate culture is created *by design* with key elements within the environment: (1) commitment and desire, (2) networking and storytelling, and (3) recognition and understanding. You'll see exactly what each of these looks like, why they're important, and how you can bring them alive in your school.

Chapters 2, 4, and 6 demonstrate the power of passion by using real stories from the field. Each of these chapters includes two **stories** with **Key Takeaways**. You'll hear from leaders who are doing the work as you read the words on this page. Each of these chapters (2, 4, and 6) also comes with two **Technical Tips.** The first of the two tips incorporates *How-Tos* that reveal the practical next steps for leaders, and the second of the two technical tips is about hiring practices and strategies so that your passionate leadership efforts are sustainable for the future. We cover topics including professional learning experiences, systems of teacher feedback, unique contributions that will amaze you, authentic teacher leadership examples, ways to celebrate using teacher-reported grades, and how extracurriculars might be the answer to student achievement. We provide a fun visual in Chapters 2, 4, and 6 as well because we believe that models, as visual representation of any content, augment the focus.

Every chapter ends with **Reflection Questions** so that you can take inventory and take action right away. We want you to think, plan, and then do something new and different for the people you lead.

The Conclusion is an action-oriented reflection activity and self-assessment, something you can use on your own or with your team. There's no better way to think into the future than to assess the present. You have to know yourself, know your current culture, and respond accordingly.

WHO SHOULD READ THIS BOOK?

Anyone with passion for student success, teaching and learning, and leadership should read this book. Most specifically, school principals, assistant principals, and district leaders should read this book and consider using it for a book study. Our hope is that this book reaches the hands of people who are current leaders but especially all the people preparing future leaders through leadership pipeline programs, colleges, and universities. Lastly, we believe that this work should permeate the community beyond the school walls. Our goal is to reach business leaders and public officials, including CEOs and elected civil servants. We contend that our message regarding passionate leadership can be the fuel for the future of our economy, our productivity as a nation, and our position on what it means to make a contribution to the world.

Acknowledgments and Dedication

We first want to acknowledge our family and close friends. Without the support we have from our wives, kids, parents, in-laws, brothers, sisters, and all of the family who surround us, we couldn't do this work. Without them, it simply wouldn't be possible to write and contribute beyond our daily work. We are forever grateful for their love and endless encouragement.

We would be remiss if we didn't thank our Delaware peers and coworkers. Delaware teachers, school leaders, and district administrators are the best in the world. Delaware school systems include urban, rural, and suburban schools with the need for passion and care at every level and in every part of the state. Because of the small nature of our great state, we know folks from north to south and east to west who are serving kids, growing as leaders, working hard, and keeping it positive every single day. We are proud of our partners in all of our Delaware schools.

We want to thank our contributors. We found stories on Twitter and Facebook, in schools we've visited, from people who reached out, and in every facet of our learning networks. The amazing, new, and different things that passionate leaders are doing for kids is beyond what we expected. The stories brought us to laughter and tears and inspired us to do more in our own roles. This book wouldn't be nearly as exciting as it is without the words that were shared with us from the people who are doing such great things for students around the world. We salute you.

Finally, this work is dedicated to anyone and everyone who is passionate about educating young people in any type of school—private, public, charter, home. Our desire is to unite our community through the love that we all have for seeing to it that the next generation and the one after that are set up for success. We care deeply about children and what it means to breathe life into a school and community so that everyone can experience a culture of devotion and respect through a true desire to get better by growing faster, contributing more with new ideas, and staying positive to support one another. If you're passionate about doing this work, we're with you in heart, mind, and spirit.

PUBLISHER'S ACKNOWLEDGMENTS

Corwin gratefully acknowledges the contributions of the following reviewers:

Elizabeth Alvarez
Chief of Schools
Chicago, IL

Scott Bailey
Associate Professor
Nacogdoches, TX

David G. Daniels
High School Principal
Conklin, NY

Louis Lim
Vice Principal, Secondary School
Richmond Hill, ON, Canada

Brigitte Tennis
Headmistress and Eighth-Grade Teacher
Redmond, WA

About the Authors

Dr. Salome Thomas-EL has been a teacher and principal in Philadelphia, PA and Wilmington, DE since 1987. He is currently the Head of School at Thomas Edison Public Charter School in Wilmington, DE. Thomas-EL received national acclaim as a teacher and chess coach at Vaux Middle School, where his students have gone on to win world recognition as Eight-Time National Chess Champions. Principal EL was a regular contributor on "The Dr. Oz Show" and the author of the best-selling books, *I Choose to Stay* and *The Immortality of Influence (Foreword by Will Smith)*. The Walt Disney Company optioned the movie rights to *I Choose to Stay.* Thomas-EL speaks to groups across the country and frequently appears on C-SPAN, CNN, and NPR Radio. He has received the Marcus A. Foster Award as the outstanding School District Administrator in Philadelphia and the University of Pennsylvania's distinguished Martin Luther King Award. Reader's Digest Magazine recognized Principal EL as an "Inspiring American Icon" and he has appeared on Oprah Radio!

Dr. Joseph Jones is Director of Assessment and Accountability, overseeing teacher effectiveness and student achievement in the New Castle County Vocational-Technical School District in Delaware. Joe is a former high school social studies teacher, assistant principal, and principal. As principal, he was named the Delaware Secondary Principal of the Year and during his tenure, Delcastle Technical High School was the first high school to receive the state's Outstanding Academic Achievement Award. He received his doctorate from the University of Delaware in educational leadership and was awarded the outstanding doctoral student award of his class. Currently, Joe works closely with local and state leaders on student achievement and accountability and has spearheaded an aggressive and successful campaign to ensure student success. Joe is also an adjunct professor, teaching and designing curriculum, both at the undergraduate and graduate levels for various universities. He presents nationally on topics of school leadership and is the co-founder of the leadership development institute, TheSchoolHouse302. Along with T.J. Vari, he co-authored *Candid and Compassionate Feedback: Transforming Everyday Practice in Schools.*

Dr. T.J. Vari is Assistant Superintendent of Secondary Schools and District Operations in the Appoquinimink School District, the fastest growing school district in Delaware. He is a former middle school assistant principal and principal and former high school English teacher and department chair. His master's degree is in school leadership and his doctorate is in innovation and leadership where he accepted an Award for Academic Excellence given to one doctoral student per graduating class. He holds several honors and distinctions, including his past appointment as President of the Delaware Association for School Administrators, his work with the Delaware Association for School Principals, and the honor in accepting the Paul Carlson Administrator of the Year Award in 2015. His efforts span beyond the K–12 arena into higher education where he holds adjunct appointments at three universities, teaching courses at the masters and doctoral level. He is a national presenter on topics of school leadership and the cofounder of TheSchoolHouse302, a leadership development institute. Along with Joe Jones, he co-authored *Candid and Compassionate Feedback: Transforming Everyday Practice in Schools.*

Introduction

Fueling the Passion in Our Schools

This book was born from many long discussions between the authors that concluded with the notion that if schools were filled with passionate staff members—teachers and leaders—then our students would be much better off. We often wondered during these conversations why the profession seems to be suffering from a passion deficit. As school and district leaders, we know it certainly is not because our fellow educators entered the profession without sparks of enthusiasm and the desire to change the world through the students we influence. That's simply not the case. In fact, many educators are so incredibly passionate that their zest is palpable. There are educators who are filled with and driven by passion throughout their entire careers. They are examples to us, and they model how this work is a way of life, not just a job, a career, or even a calling. As we delved into this topic, through dinner table conversations and friendly chatter, we always came back to the teachers who truly made a difference in our lives, not only for what they knew but for how they made us feel—inspired, confident, able, with a clear sense of self, and belonging. Joe clearly recalls a time on the school playground during picture day when a teacher he didn't know walked over, said "Hi" and commented, "I really like that shirt." Joe was feeling a little insecure because the shirt was not what a typical 11-year-old would wear, but it was all he had. What the teacher didn't know is that Joe's dad had left that year, abandoning him, his older brother, older sister, and their mom who was struggling to keep things afloat. That day, ingrained in Joe's mind forever, is inspiration that kind words and pure good will always make a difference. What's more is that you

1

never know who may need it. This is what still drives Joe, today, as an educator, like so many of us who have similar stories to tell.

What we realize, though, is that we need more passionate educators to make the great strides that we have before us. Our goal with this book is to fuel the passion for those who are still running strong but also to reignite the passion that many of us once had for serving children. We desire to motivate the educational community, and others, to strive to become the best teachers and leaders we can be. It is time for us to support and inspire leaders, with boots on the ground, who are committed to taking courageous actions for student success and well-being. This book is a call to action for teachers and leaders around the world to recommit to becoming the passionate educators that our children deserve. Furthermore, passion is important in every industry. This book can serve as a reminder for anyone in any profession.

Why are we in such a critical need for passion in schools? The answer is that the school systems designed to educate our youth don't do a good enough job nurturing educators. Our schools don't always encourage the qualities that are needed for people to be passionate and maintain that passion throughout their careers. Instead, more often than we would like, our current educational system unfortunately does the opposite. But we know it doesn't have to be that way. We've built cultures in schools where passion was the norm—in public and private schools, in elementary schools, in middle schools, in high schools, in charter schools, and in career and technical schools. We've brought the passion with us into a school, and we've watched as others have rekindled their passion for teaching and learning. Because we see such a critical need, we put together a blueprint for any school to follow, and if they follow the script to the letter, they will reignite the passion in the people who work there. Principals will need to walk through their schools with a water hose because their staffs will be on fire for children.

We hope this book will inspire you to smile and laugh about some of our current conditions but to also have hope for a brighter future. We want to spark innovation, creativity, and new ways of thinking about how we build culture in schools, and we hope you'll take immediate and powerful action with us on a new journey across the country and around the world. For those of us in the trenches who know so well that school systems are ready for a new approach and innovative thinking, this book is our blueprint for unparalleled success in our schools. We know that you have a passion, a spark for kids and adults, or you wouldn't be reading this book, but we're going to fuel that even further through positivity. We're going to inspire you to lead others to grow faster, and we're going to show you how a collective commitment in your school will raise the roof. In fact, we are demanding that you join our revolution. We know you can make this happen in your school and district, but we also know that there are distinct challenges that you will need to overcome.

We could spend the entire book identifying and admiring the problems that exist in schools where passion is low or even non-existent—but that would do nothing more than criticize schools and educators working in them, playing the blame game. That's not the book we want to write, nor is it a book we are interested in reading, and we're sure you feel the same. There's already enough blame for everyone in our profession to have two helpings and then go back for a third. We won't do any blaming here because we believe that if you're not part of the solution, you're just adding to the problem. In fact, this book is a call to action for educators to make sure that passion is in our schools, for our students, for the teachers, and for the administrators, all doing the work that it takes to be the beacon of hope for our future. However, to understand how to increase our passion to new levels in schools, we must always be aware of the systemic issues we face before our solutions are understood. We will take a moment in this introduction to recognize three of the most crippling obstacles, which act as roadblocks and hazards when firing up the passion engines in our schools. We call them *Trip Traps* because they end up tripping you up and trapping your thinking, preventing you from moving forward. These issues are an affront to your leadership, in the classroom and beyond, and you must be courageous to move past them. Despite these obstacles and challenges we note here, many school leaders are currently making it happen, and their inspirational message and scores of achievement can be replicated. Their stories are found in this book, written for you to spur you on in your journey as an educator. And this blueprint will show you how to make great things happen for your school as well, but let's be sure to outline the issues we will encounter along the way.

TRIP TRAPS: COMMON TRAPS THAT TRIP UP EVEN THE BEST LEADERS

Trip Trap #1: The Education System Tends to Major in the Minor. School districts, for too long, have focused on things that teachers and school leaders know are not what gets the real work done for kids, and their voice is lost at the decision-making table, wherever that may be. Policies like No Child Left Behind, Race to the Top, and even the Every Student Succeeds Act put a ton of inappropriately applied pressure on schools that doesn't take into consideration what really matters most. We're not advocating for lower accountability measures, and we're not policy experts, but we do know that policies often mandate a different focus than what is needed, too often treating symptoms and not the core issues. When educators are empowered to put first things first, to create a plan that truly homes in on the priorities of a school, they stretch far beyond test scores to create systems that are successful at more than "proficiency."

Recent educational policies have turned improvement measures into pressure cookers, and the result is compliance-based thinking about how to help teachers get better and push schools to stay on track toward success. All the while, we're thumbing through hand-books to follow the rules to document our progress, and, in turn, we lose focus on what matters most. It's why we hear a lot of educators question "Is this what's best for kids?" In a system where decisions don't always get made with that in mind, it's the right thing to ask, but it means that we arrived at a time where a decision might get made that's not best for kids. Not good, and it's time to make sweeping changes to our blueprint for sustaining passion in our schools. Let's be ready to prioritize so compliance doesn't compete with making a difference for our kids.

Time spent on anything except a deep desire to grow is time wasted in schools. The system of accountability is broken when it doesn't support growth and development, and we want to bring that sentiment back. We'll show you how to spark passion and the desire to grow faster in Part I.

> The kind of inspiration that uplifts people, organizations, and communities is more than an idle wish or fancy speech; it must also instigate powerful, new, and deliberate actions. It is evident in what people do as well as what they say, and requires courage, daring, and determination to bring it to fruition. (Hargreaves, Boyle, & Harris, 2014)

Trip Trap #2: The Load Is Far Too Heavy for Only a Few to Carry Its Weight. The weight of educating young people is not getting any lighter and will likely only get heavier. The only way to lighten the load in the future is if we all contribute to carrying its weight. Too often we've heard seasoned teachers tell new teachers that "It gets easier after your first year." They say this to new teachers as a way to make them feel better after a bad day or a difficult week. But the reality is that it only gets easier when teachers grow and master their craft. In fact, we contend that this type of thinking doesn't recognize and appreciate the incredible growth teachers experience over a career. The truth is that the work never gets easier. Rather, seasoned teachers get better over time. Yes, you may develop systems and structures that free up some time or give the foundation for great lessons, but great teachers then use that time to improve other areas, become more creative, and strive to reach every child. They grow, they learn, and they develop into masters of their craft, making the work seemingly easier when it's not, and it shouldn't be.

We have to be mindful of telling ourselves that teaching should be, or will become, easier. It may seem like semantics, but this way of thinking actually assumes that the load is too much to bear: "Don't worry it will get easier." What we need to actually say that empowers teachers is, "Don't worry, you're going to get much better." Teacher retention is a major concern, and in one study by the Bill & Melinda Gates Foundation, teachers acknowledged that they need *supportive leadership* and *time to collaborate* with their peers (Scholastic, 2011). Education is a demanding profession and it's not easy work. We have to quit praying for a lighter load and start building a stronger back. That only happens through supportive environments, collaboration, partnerships, and placing value on hard work. The view that teaching is an innate skill, and that good teachers were "born" to teach, erodes the technical, scientific, and skill-driven side of the profession. Education is not an early-out, summers-off, no-nights type of work that some believe it to be. Great educators strive to perfect their craft, and it is vital that this is recognized and rewarded, which has to happen strategically from the inside out.

On top of that, we tend to move people through the system without proper preparation. A good teacher becomes an assistant principal. A good assistant principal becomes a principal. A good principal becomes an assistant superintendent. A good assistant superintendent becomes a superintendent. Education promotes from within, based on prior effectiveness, moving people into positions that they may have no experience or aptitude to do. It's no different than if a good architect becomes the CEO in a large architecture firm, finding himself working in a position that he is ill-equipped to do. There's evidence that some of our teachers aren't totally prepared for the classroom as they leave their preservice programs, and yet we operate in a system that promotes people based on degrees, certifications, and years of service and not always the ability to do the job. It's possible that someone moves all the way to the highest levels within the school system without the proper support and preparation needed to fulfill the responsibilities. We need to work in a model that supports those in their current roles and develops them to meet the needs of the organization and their future aspirations. Working extremely hard, fingers-to-the-bone, is what it takes, along with a contribution from everyone.

It's imperative that "work ethic," with everyone contributing, is at the heart of our conversations about hiring and retaining the right people in our schools who in turn inspire our students to persevere despite the odds. We have to ensure that people are set up for success in the work environment, but we need to set the bar high enough that people realize that this profession demands a great deal of time, talent, and expertise. A few cannot carry the many. Schools require everyone within the school community to work together for the betterment of children. We need educators who are willing to take control of the steering wheel, leaders who are not comfortable just being passengers. We need the willing and the brave to take the wheel and drive forward, pushing our organizations toward excellence at all costs. Our schools, our students, cannot afford to carry passengers among us, simply along for the ride. We can't continue to enable riders, and we need to value our drivers——those willing to take command amid uncertainty and fear. One way to value these drivers is to recognize their hard work and willingness to push forward despite the conditions. Our value for the driver will make the passengers more uncomfortable, and in a culture committed to success, the passenger's seat will get smaller and smaller in the future. This is not a call for more leaders and fewer followers; on the contrary, this is about stronger leaders and faithful followers. Too often, the passengers don't even wonder or concern themselves with the issues and traps that prevent success and progress in our schools. For this, they cannot be permitted to remain idle and at ease. In this section, you'll need to question which seat you're in and possibly make a choice and a change. If you have a desire to improve your school's passion, we have a plan for you in Part II.

Trip Trap #3: We Need to Do a Better Job of Supporting the Profession From Within. There are some schools getting it right, supporting from within, and we need to learn to replicate that across the system. To do so, there are a few overarching issues that we need to overcome that are preventing this from happening at scale. These issues are pervasive within the system itself and center on a lack of support from inside our schools and districts. Have you ever had a *cul de sac* conversation with a teacher or an assistant principal and the immediate focal point was the most basic and worst of all situations from their day? It's normal. We justify it as venting, but, it's too bad, too often, and too detrimental that our method for dealing with the stress is our need to share the stories from our work day that highlight our lowest moments. These stories create a false perception of the reality in our schools and depict only the negative narrative from within them.

There are the inevitable minute-by-minute challenges in schools, but among 101 of our stories from any given day, there are

100 positive, but our *need* to revert to the single negative story accentuates the negative. This is precisely part of the trap. It over-shadows the good and crushes positive thinking about our own work environment and schools in general, and that comes from those within the system. The good news is that it's reversible. We can flip this need to focus on the negative with a desire to share the positive and create a culture of celebration. One incredible educator who we've had the privilege of working with, Glenn Veit of Meredith Middle School, is famous for replying to those who ask about his day, by saying, "Overall, I had a great day. In fact, I've never really had a bad day, bad moments, but not an entire day." Glenn is notoriously positive, and when asked how he is doing, he replies "I'm always good." When pressed about being "always good," he says, "sure, there are things that aren't good, but overall, I'm good." It's this kind of outlook that's necessary to paint the appropriate picture of the real sentiment from within our schools.

Not only do we tend to highlight the negative from within, we also tend to feel like many situations are out of our control, so we cast blame or throw our hands up in the air and accept the distorted notion that we can't do anything about it. We know of passionate educators, though, who pursue their vision without falter and face these issues head on by building a network of support within and beyond the walls of the school. For example, teacher quality and teacher shortages are a common problem schools face. We've all heard it before: "There aren't enough quality educators out there." But passionate leaders committed to building great schools know how to attract people and take advantage of every opportunity to hire and retain incredible educators. They do anything from develop-ing in-house teacher preparation programs to working with sur-rounding universities to building relationships with local chambers of commerce to petitioning local legislators for pipelines of possibili-ties. Great schools make this a community issue and not just a school issue. They don't just believe in shaking their heads at the problem, but rather shaking hands with people who can help solve them. The difference is that passionate educators don't just admire problems, which only leads to apathy and procrastination, they pursue answers and solutions with vigor and resolve. With so many pressures from the outside, we have to be our own advocates and sources of strength for the sake of ourselves, our teachers, and our students. We need to provide a positive charge for every single school in the United States and around the world.

Finally, we need kids not only to understand the power of learning, but to see their teachers and administrators as role models and great ambassadors of the profession. Students need to view the profession as something fun and inspiring to do when they grow up. When we lack this view of ourselves, we deplete our own worth and value in our roles, and it doesn't demonstrate to kids that teaching is a noble profession and unbelievably thrilling and enjoyable work. Teaching kids a new concept, fostering ideas about themselves and the world is so exciting that we want the joy and power of teaching and learning to come through these pages and shake you as the reader. We want this passion and understanding of the uniqueness and power of the profession to be the mantra of what we demonstrate to kids on a daily basis. We owe it to ourselves and to the future of teaching and learning in America and around the world.

OUR MANTRAS

This book is set up as a recipe, identifying the right ingredients for tackling tough problems in schools so that you can reignite the winning passion that the best schools in our nation exude from the inside out. This book does not simply tout heralded best practices or suggest strategic planning, it features real people with real stories about how it's being done in schools today. This work encompasses the attitudes needed among everyone and the culture that must exist in order for best practices and strategic plans to be effective.

We have three mantras that we abide by to inspire passion in ourselves. They are easy to use and powerful when followed consistently over and over again. Figure I.1 shows how all three mantras work together to encompass one cohesive model of action.

1. *Today* I will grow by challenging myself to be the best I can.

2. *Today* I will work harder than yesterday because there isn't anything more important than now.

3. *Today* I will lift people through positivity.

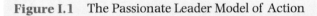

Figure I.1 The Passionate Leader Model of Action

We believe that if every educator says these three phrases at the start of every day, at the start of every class period, at the start of every meeting, and whenever they are about to encounter something new or difficult, the profession will be fueled with passion. The mantras spell out a recipe for success that any school can use to inspire people to be passionate.

Part I

Inspiring to Grow

A Culture of Strong Relationships

"If you hear a voice within you say, 'you can't paint,' then by all means paint and that voice will be silenced."

—Van Gogh

Our strengths come to bear when we are thriving within a school culture, among a group of educators who are fully committed to their own growth and who seek out opportunities to become better. Passionate educators take full responsibility for their own development, and they seek to learn and grow each day for the betterment of their students. They embrace the mantra that *Today I will grow by challenging myself to be the best I can.* They know that within a diverse and challenging environment, every single day holds new situations with the promise that they truly can make a difference in the lives of children. Challenging ourselves means seeking out new horizons, reaching for new ideas, uncovering greater possibilities for discovery and development. This runs counter to a culture that stifles new meaning and which fails to recognize our infinite potential to experience growth. Because the ultimate goal is for all students to succeed, all educators must be willing to master their craft, pursuing their expertise with a fervor to excel and to implement the best teaching practices in a supportive, growth-oriented culture. It's the stories we tell, like the one about Principal Cynthia Jewell, that reinforce our work and remind us that change is difficult but achievable. When a passionate group of committed adults rally behind a noble purpose, success is inevitable.

Results Through Passionate Leadership
Inspiring Change and Reaching Goals Through Data Consciousness and Difficult Conversations

Principal Cynthia Jewell, Stockbridge Elementary Stockbridge, Georgia

We live in a society that relies mostly on using assessments and test scores to measure and report how well our schools are doing. Whether we are looking at state, national, or international assessments, they all are commonly used to rate, compare, and assign a grade to our schools. Much of the standardized assessment narrative is that schools aren't doing well, and Stockbridge Elementary found itself in this same boat. Interestingly, at one time, the school was performing very well and receiving tremendous accolades. However, as the state test changed, and rigor increased, scores did not. Stockbridge was left in need of revitalization with the ultimate demand to overhaul their practices.

Even though state assessments are only one indicator of performance and aren't always the right reason to react with sweeping changes, they do indicate student performance on the standards and can't be ignored over time. For Stockbridge, the numbers were low and stagnant. As administration changed, the new principal, Cynthia Jewell, came to the school with a fresh outlook. She wanted Stockbridge to excel academically, in all areas, and she was eager to build a community obsessed with student achievement.

Quickly in her tenure, Principal Jewell identified groups of students who were not doing well. She dug into the data and realized that her response to intervention (RTI) Tier 2 and Tier 3 students stood out as not making the necessary gains toward proficiency. Knowing these students were already receiving assistance within the school, she questioned what else they might be able to do to solve the problem. Identifying the students who are in need is actually the easy part; figuring out what to do to solve the student achievement puzzle is the true challenge. As a result, she realized that to make a difference, the faculty had to accept that the scores weren't necessarily a student issue, but rather one that everyone needed to own. The staff had to take full responsibility for student learning. She asked the question, "Are we satisfied with our current practices and how poorly our students are doing?" One major conclusion they made was about lesson planning. Although efficient, the grade-level teams used group-made lesson plans that divided up the subjects by content area and then shared them prior to teaching the particular lesson. The lessons were aligned to the standards, but this divide-and-conquer approach left teachers without clarity on what they were teaching and the lessons were not instructionally responsive to all students' needs. The plans were too generic and lacked input.

As a result, Stockbridge embarked on a new journey to improve how teachers collaborated, to institute formalized professional learning communities (PLCs), and to implement an aggressive reading initiative. Principal Jewell emphasized to everyone, "If the students cannot read, they simply cannot learn." They underwent intensive professional development, which was then reinforced in PLCs and during walkthroughs. Frequent visits to classrooms were conducted by the administration and the instructional coach, specifically designed to see the initiative in action and how well the teachers were doing. The first year had its challenges, but they knew going in that change always takes place after conflict.

During the second year, the initiative started to take hold, and teacher buy-in spiked. They began to take real ownership of the new student learning targets. They reimagined the importance of their instruction, their ability to connect with kids, and their enthusiasm for the work. Of course, as with all change initiatives, it wasn't easy, but the only alternative was accepting failure. Instead, they pushed forward; formative assessments were used throughout lessons and within units, aligned to benchmarks to determine ongoing progress. They saw results. Students who were once unsuccessful were growing and, and in some cases, exceeding their goals.

Unfortunately, new endeavors are often riddled with challenges and resistance. For many, change is difficult and creates discomfort, which in Stockbridge's case, led to a 40 percent teacher turnover by the end of Cynthia's second year with the program. This exodus could easily be misconstrued by placing blame on Cynthia for

(Continued)

(Continued)

alienating her staff, ignoring the need for strong relationships, and demonstrating poor leadership. Cynthia herself could have doubted her decisions, questioning her actions. However, the reality was that the changes were making a difference, and some of the turnover was a good thing. PLCs were starting to function well, and teacher leaders were stepping forward to make contributions to the changes with a revived sense of purpose and passion. Those who weren't willing to change felt the pressure of what it means to hold onto the past when everything around you is transforming. Fortunately, the turnover was an opportunity for new people to shine, and it gave liberty to Cynthia to hire teachers, fully committed to student success, with the mindset that as professionals they too will learn and grow every day.

Teachers who know that their impact is making a difference coupled with improved student outcomes creates a culture where everyone is learning together. With energy, passion, and excitement, the teachers were now willing to be coached, visited by other teachers, and engaged in a cycle of growth. The school continues to experience gains, and the teachers are now leading the way. Cynthia's new goals take into consideration even higher levels of student performance, and she knows that it means doing even more than they have so far, in new and different ways, with growth opportunities for everyone.

Cynthia is intent that Stockbridge will continue to succeed, and as the community continues to change, they will be ready to meet the needs of everyone who walks through their doors. She is creating a culture that champions the students and their success, regardless of their background or economic status. She ended the interview with resolve. She said that despite the school being high poverty, "how a child eats [free-and-reduced lunch] will not determine how well they learn." What we love about this story is Cynthia's commitment to building a learning culture for both students and staff. It's clear that under Cynthia's leadership everyone came to accept the importance of their own growth. A committed staff who takes ownership of student success through unique contributions and a strong commitment to learn and grow is the essence of passionate leadership.

A Learning Culture, Not a Teaching Culture

"The culture of a workplace—an organization's values, norms, and practices—has a huge impact on our happiness and success."

—Adam Grant, *Originals*, 2016

EVERYONE WORKS TO LEARN

A model learning environment is a space of contentment, comfort, and value with an extreme focus on learning. It's vibrant and radiates positive activity grounded in an emotional connection between the students and teachers. When students are actively engaged with the content, one another, and the teacher, it's literally palpable. A model learning environment is one where the students direct their own learning within the context that the teacher created, and the teacher facilitates as a guide and a coach. In classrooms where learning is taking place at the highest level, teachers move around purposefully, offering feedback to students, clarifying misconceptions, checking for understanding, and asking students to think deeply. Perhaps a supervisor is even in the room, observing the nuances of the class, identifying high-leverage strategies that should be praised and reinforced, uncovering opportunities for tweaks and adjustments to the lesson with specific feedback to improve performance. Everyone is working to support the learning that is clearly taking place.

The classroom described above is a model to support a culture of learning. It is alive and filled with passion that can be felt by everyone in the room, and it distinguishes the various roles that each person plays, whether they are a student, teacher, or supervisor. Although the roles among those in the classroom may differ—students learning, teachers teaching, and supervisors observing—each individual contributes to the overall achievement taking place. The student, teacher, and supervisor each focus on learning, growing, and using best practices in various ways to support one another. It means that students are taking responsibility for their own learning and growth, teachers are working toward student mastery, and supervisors are supporting the learning process for everyone. This is how great classrooms function and it's what the larger school community recognizes as excellence from their schools. We all want classrooms where student learning is recognizable, where risk-taking among students and teachers is encouraged and rewarded, and where expectations are rooted in accountability and support. Just like the classroom we describe, schools and school systems need to operate in this type of ongoing support and collaboration among all involved to develop the "collective capacity" for improved student achievement and increased levels of learning (Fullan, 2011b). It has to be true for the students, true for the teachers, and true for the leaders.

The reality, though, is that it takes many different people and organizations within the broader context of education to work to achieve our desired results in schools. The first question, then, becomes whether or not we know and understand the "best practices" necessary for success and even whether or not we fundamentally agree on them as practitioners. And, when we're not reaching our desired outcomes for students, the second question simply becomes: why aren't these agreed upon best practices a more common occurrence? To understand the reasons why these questions arise, we need to explore how education gets muddy and how many viable practices are slowed down and rendered ineffective. One reason is that education gets messy when we become entangled in what we call the instructional-*ations*—stipulations, articulations, regulations, and legislation. On the surface, these teaching and learning efforts are not a bad thing, and many are well meaning, intended to solve real problems, but too often they interfere with our focus.

One of the major challenges that school systems face is in how the typical changes trickle down to the people on the frontlines—teachers, specialists, paraprofessionals, and administrators. Too often, by the time the "new ideas" are presented to the staff, even with a solid rationale, it is often perceived as just "one more thing," and it's reduced to a directive from on high. We recognize that change is common and should be positive, with many efforts designed to improve conditions, but that change initiatives in schools are generally negatively received. This perception isn't wrong or even unique to education. The health care industry is a great example of a system that has significant oversight from government regulators, including agencies such as the Department of Justice, the Office of Inspector General, and the U.S. Food and Drug Administration, all of which are in place to "protect the public." As a result, the health care industry, and its various components, are constantly subject to regulations and change initiatives beyond the immediate control of the people doing the work within the industry.

Many of the intended reforms fall into what Fullan (2011b) described as "wrong drivers." These reforms include "punitive accountability versus capacity building . . . or ad hoc versus systemic policies" (Fullan, 2011b). To break this down further, the issue that schools often face is that the "regulatory" changes directly impact the classroom without additional support or resources for implementation. Over time, increased mandates without support, along with a negative narrative that schools are failing, can reduce the excitement and passion among those in the field. To exacerbate the problem, these changes are piled on top of one another so rapidly that the people in the trenches don't have time to fully grasp the true intent of the reform efforts and, therefore, cannot successfully implement the new ideas with fidelity. In an industry where the practitioners rely on passion, combined with expertise, the changes inadvertently restrict and constrain the work. The real detriment when this happens is that the passion and fire within the educator can slowly extinguish. The teacher becomes someone who dreads meetings and visits from district office personnel because the information and messaging are essentially the same: "What we're doing is never enough." Whether it's introducing new regulations and mandates, unpacking new or additional state assessments, reworking how the school can improve to meet new targets, or affirming additional responsibilities beyond the classroom, the changes blur together and feed a level of hopelessness that reduces the commitment toward the changes to compliance and an attitude of just "tell me what I need to do." At their worst, the instructional-*ations* erode educators' sense of professionalism to the point that they devolve into automatons, delivering a program while feeling personally devalued. The fact is, the opposite should be true. Educators should be passionate people who are held in high regard because of their unique expertise to teach children and shape the future generations of our workforce. And when we're all not working together to support the learning culture in our schools, students suffer.

UNINTENDED CONSEQUENCES

So much work among well-intended reformers has been done to elevate expectations, increase rigor, and provide guidance throughout all of our schools. These efforts illuminate areas of need and increase the cry for all children to receive the very best education that can be provided. In the wake of these efforts, though, exist people who don't perceive themselves as part of the equation in their creation, the success they boast, or the solutions they propose, but rather a part of the systemic educational problems that they highlight. We don't foresee this style of reform changing—nor will its consequences. Actually, it's better to be accepted as the new normal and for educational influencers and school leaders to do everything in their power to instill passion as the fuel for fervor and commitment to a learning culture so that we can thrive in a system that is constantly changing. When combined with technical expertise, passionate leaders create incredible learning environments for teachers and students to reach new heights. Outside the walls of the school, there are also a number of efforts designed to create a better system, but both internal and external efforts need to be in sync for either to be successful.

Unfortunately, this is too often not the case. However, to realize the desired results, schools must be empowered and given a solid foundation of support through professional learning experiences and quality feedback to improve practice. In a learning culture, growth is the only mechanism to battle constant change, and many school systems are beginning to get it right. The unintended consequences of the outside-in reform efforts can only be mitigated through professional growth and a desire to improve the system from the inside out to meet each and every new demand placed on schools.

Due to competing efforts and initiatives, school leaders must view leading their school system through bifocal lenses. The first, an internal lens, drives progress and change based on key data that the school and district leaders have available and know they must act upon. Especially where equity is questionable, leaders have to confront and alter current scenarios. This information drives professional learning and growth experiences to make the necessary improvements internally. The second, an external lens, anticipates influences from outside the immediate school system that may also drive change. These "outside the school" changes also require extensive professional development and growth opportunities so that our capacity for the work deepens and our ability to manage change increases. Skilled leaders must learn how to manage both types of change to equip their systems by aligning all of the moving internal and external parts. This alignment reframes change as a holistic approach and seeks to reduce burdens through meaningful opportunities for professional learning and growth. Ensuring that every aspect of the organization operates in harmony through the two-lens approach will fight the belief that educators are the casualties of constant change; it will anticipate needs before they arise and it will increase the awareness of the necessity for professional growth. Through systems thinking, the unintended consequences of reform efforts can be alleviated for a unified approach to a learning culture.

AN ALIGNED SYSTEM OF IMPROVEMENT

Student achievement has become synonymous with reform and standardization. Name the reform, and not too far down the line, you'll find how it is designed to lead to student success through clearer standards. The goal of reform is to make improvements; to ensure that these improvements have a chance to stick, it is necessary to align all of the pieces and parts together in harmony. Alignment among interdependent parts is critical for effectiveness and overall success. The term *alignment*, within education, typically focuses on the *Big Four*—standards, curriculum, instruction, and assessments—with standards serving as the primary guiding force. The belief is that the alignment of these components is critical if we desire to make educationally informed decisions, improve the overall system, and educate toward mastery. For the most part, this is accurate and serves as much of the foundational premise behind the standards-based movement. As Resnick, Rothman, Slattery, and Vranick (2002) indicate, "the theory behind standards-based education holds that standards should be rigorous and challenging, and that they should be specific enough to guide both teachers' and students' day-to-day work and the development of tests." Although this movement has evolved over the years, raising questions about depth of knowledge, grade-level placement, and teacher efficacy, the goal remains the same. The core of the work is to identify clear standards and align the key areas of learning within the system to achieve them. In fact, one of the guiding principles for the Common Core State Standards was to establish a baseline of proficiency, clarified for each grade level and within each state (Common Core State Standards, 2018).

Unfortunately, overall alignment within the educational system is complex, and coordinating efforts to maximize effectiveness of any alignment effort is challenging. One reason, as Martone and Sireci (2009) point out, is that alignment refers to different areas within education and "assessment, standards, and instruction are all integral to student achievement, but they have each been enacted at multiple levels of the educational structure." And, at times, their enactment within the system is done with a lack of consideration for one another. These various structures create unique circumstances because the change initiatives, whether through policy, legislative reform, or even district informed decision-making, may not fully calculate the distinct influence they have over the classroom environment or, most importantly, the supports that are needed for actual advancements to take place. Change requires realignment of the processes, but too often the realignment doesn't delve into the human side of the equation. It focuses on the processes but not the people. We tend to take for granted the instructor side of the instructional equation, assuming that if standards, curriculum, and assessments are aligned, so too will be the instruction. That's simply not the case unless we professionally develop the people and provide frequent measures of feedback for their growth. It may sound strange but education isn't generally considered to be a "people business" as often as it should. If we want passion, we have to think about the people and how they fit into every change effort within a learning culture. If the system is not aligned, improvements will not stick.

Businesses and schools, or any organization for that matter, are really no different in terms of making changes and supporting the people. Organizations are made up of many moving parts that all serve specific and necessary functions. If one part is misaligned, the entire organization suffers. The alignment among the Big Four is critical, however, so that educators fully understand the changes needed and that they're reflected in practice. That's precisely why the alignment process is crucial to success. Stakeholders don't have a problem identifying the failing parts and then legislating, influencing, or implementing new ideas or policies. The challenge is in seeing to it that true reform takes hold at the classroom level. The alignment has to take hold for the people doing the work, the ones who will actually transfer the change into a deliverable experience for students. This is why professional learning and feedback systems are needed because they are the primary methods we have to bolster understanding and expertise, and they need to be done in new and different ways with greater frequency and a stronger sense of urgency. Change initiatives require extensive follow through with ongoing and sustainable support to fully equip teachers and administrators on the frontlines.

For alignment to occur, and for it to truly galvanize all of the components of the organization, it cannot stop with just the structures and systems. It must encompass the people, the educators, in a culture of learning and support. To fully implement any change initiative involving the Big Four, we must combine them with what we call the *Powerful Two*—professional development and instructional feedback. The first is about creating powerful learning experiences for educators, and the second is about cranking up the frequency and quality of feedback and coaching to harness the power that comes with praise and criticism. Anything short of this simply creates what we call a *teaching culture*, which is not the same as a *learning culture*. A culture whereby teachers are not at the helm of the teaching and learning, delivering instruction without fully understanding or embracing the power or intent behind any given reform or change, is what we deem a *teaching culture*. This limits their ownership, their connectedness with the profession, and the passion that ignites their creativity and inspires students. A *learning culture* is much different; it's a place where we grow as teachers and leaders from the inside out. It's a system that is truly aligned and ready for change.

GROWTH FROM THE INSIDE OUT

The good news is that growth, albeit seemingly put upon educators, can happen from within the school system (Elmore, 2004) if we're willing to look at things differently than we have in the past. We somehow arrived at a time when professional development and feedback aren't exciting and fun, which is what we need to change if we're going to become a real learning culture. There are a number of reasons for this but one is that even though "instruction" is commonly discussed during reform efforts, it tends to take a back seat to the alignment of standards with curriculum. What ends up happening is that we lose focus on developing teachers and enabling them to perfect their craft during the change. Instead of growing the people, we deliver a new program to them.

Kirsch, Bildner, and Walker (2016) tell *Harvard Business Review* readers that for solutions to organizational issues to work, "systems entrepreneurs must have a deep understanding of the system or systems they are trying to change and all the factors that shape it." In other words, leaders need a deep understanding of their systems to implement new solutions to problems that may, in fact, be caused by the system itself. Education is no different and to develop a learning culture, the changes must confront the causes of the problem, be sustainable, and supported. This creates a culture where the educators can take full ownership of their performance, learning, and outcomes. In addition, school leaders must incorporate methodologies to fully calculate the toll that the change will take on the school and its staff. Educational leaders can benefit from neurosurgeon McLaughlin's (2018) advice, who suggests three strategies when facing fear and stress: "1. Always place a drain; 2. Never cut what you can't see; and 3. Get a second opinion." Although the language is tailored for a doctor, it is applicable to all organizational leaders who face stress. From an educational viewpoint, these three suggestions are designed to properly manage situations when experiencing large degrees of change that tax and stress the system. Placing a drain in Dr. McLaughlin's example refers to a way to "relieve intracranial pressure" during surgery. The drain is vital in the operating room. Within education, it is critical to institute a release valve, as in to not overburden the school community, including the teaching staff and the students. Great leaders are situationally aware and know when the stress is bending the community versus breaking it. Change is needed but it only works when people are supported through a deepening of their capacity, skills, and abilities.

Even though educators aren't operating on the brain, "never cut what you can't see" implies that the problem must be fully understood before working to move or eliminate something. The implementation process must account for all of the various elements that are going to be impacted, before, during, and after the decision. And lastly, getting "additional opinions" is critical for perspective (McLaughlin, 2018). Successful school leaders understand the importance of hearing from a cross section of the staff, giving them a voice, before rolling out a new idea. This approach allows for the magnitude of the change to be calculated and measured against the current school community and what they can bear. Handled well, change can be woven into the structure of the school and implemented with fidelity. This helps to create the change and reach the goals that are desired. When teachers understand the *why* and are included in the *how*, the *what* almost never matters. When leaders obtain a 360° view of a situation, they can successfully eliminate the perception that this new thing is "one more thing," which only whittles away at passion and professionalism. What we don't want from any programmatic change is to boil the profession down to script and deliver. Educational leaders could benefit by incorporating these simple surgical strategies to manage change in a way that complements and reinforces the system without breaking the people within it.

In turn, when change management strategies are maximized, the aligned system offers ongoing high-quality professional development as the norm with frequent quality feedback, aligned to the overall goals and what is newly expected. School leaders, and others who influence what happens in the classroom, need to steer clear of the trap of believing that success is the result of initiatives and reform efforts alone. The truth is that real change always lies with the people, not the policy or the program.

School systems cannot be stifled by policies and rules that don't account for the human element of the educational system. Recognizing that passionate educators make the difference is what reframes the narrative around school reform. We fully understand the need for reforming the work to meet the demands of the future way in which we must educate young people, and this is in no way an attempt to deregulate schools or pontificate on local control. Nor is this a bash-the-standards movement. In fact, improvements are desperately needed and rigorous standards are a must in getting us there. Rather, this is a call to action that at the heart of policies there are people who need support in executing them. If the goal of the policy is to fix a problem, we contend that the policy itself will fall short every time if we don't fully equip teachers and administrators with differentiated learning experiences and quality feedback on their implementation. The growth has to happen from the inside and it requires quality level of support for the people doing the work.

QUALITY LEVELS OF SUPPORT

Once a clear understanding of the moving parts is in place, quality levels of support allow new processes to take hold for the people who are executing the initiative. As previously mentioned, many of the standards-based reforms attempt to focus on instruction by addressing alignment between standards, curriculum, and assessment but too often the instructional improvements seem prescriptive and the real learning around the new program of work is cursory. It's also important that what we call *prescriptive teaching* is not confused with *resources.* For example, giving teachers a new reading series, aligned to the standards, and offering a one-day training on the program that the teachers may not even fully buy into, is a recipe for mediocrity. Although the resource (reading program) may be of quality, the implementation will suffer from prescriptive teaching due to a lack of teacher development for using the program. When teachers accuse a resource as being prescribed in nature, it's often due to a lack of training. Again, the result is a *teaching* culture and not a *learning* culture. The changes must occur with an environment that views teacher development as important as student achievement. Schools that are passionate about student achievement invest in their teachers and build a culture where professional learning is expected and rewarded. One critical disclaimer is that this type of development is not the typical trainings that many of us have experienced. We're calling for a new push that requires professional learning to be differentiated so that educators are moving toward mastery in the art and science of teaching and learning.

There are a few different ways to achieve this environment, but it begins with empowerment and ends with accountability. Passionate leaders possess the courage to put teachers in charge of their learning, and they inspire teachers to solicit feedback on the risks that they are taking and the new practices that they are using in the classroom to engage students. Teachers all have various needs and require different levels of support. Three major mistakes that schools often make are (1) overlooking the talent within the school as a resource for professional development, (2) failing to differentiate professional development based on the experience and expertise of the teachers, and (3) forgetting to reteach and reinforce new practices for teachers who recently underwent a new training. Consider a high school with a major literacy initiative. The school's data reveals that students are underperforming with about 30 percent of the incoming freshmen reading on a sixth-grade level. This reality calls for several internal changes that are orchestrated by the administration, such as extensive professional development (PD), restructuring the master schedule to offer tiered ninth-grade ELA classes, and additional resources. To successfully address the issue, the professional development that the school offers must tap into the expertise of the current teachers. Too often, schools will look outside when the answers might be already on staff. It's always best to empower the staff to lead whenever possible. Ongoing PD throughout the year to build literacy in the content areas, as an example, is a perfect place for teacher leadership. This requires leveraging master teachers who already know how to surgically build literacy into their instruction but do so in isolation. Yes, a program may be necessary, but that would fall into the training bucket, which also requires follow up support and evaluation. Even when the PD is from an outside party, afterward, it must consistently be reinforced by the expertise that the staff can provide and feedback on the new practices. This means that even when outsiders are brought in, on staff training and development experts are appointed as leads. Imagine, in our example, that year one goes smoothly with a few identifiable issues. In year two, as the school continues the initiative, teacher leaders take the lead and offer ongoing professional learning toward mastery, ensuring the growth and sustainability of the efforts.

A school with a learning culture is sensitive to the skills and expertise of each teacher as well as the skills that need to be learned. Imagine that the same high school with the reading program has eighty teachers on staff; it's inevitable that they are all performing at differing levels. A learning-driven culture respects and knows the talents of the teachers and creates a learning environment that leverages their expertise and designs PD to ensure that they are learning the necessary skills to complement their current understanding and execution. This approach empowers teachers, respects their time, and promotes an environment where they are able to grow and develop, based on their needs and skill level.

The accountability piece of this model is that everyone is expected to learn and grow. Everyone. And the learning is directly tied to and embedded in the Powerful Two—professional development and instructional feedback. The first power is in the use of high-quality professional development for everyone. This is where teachers receive PD, based on their skills and expertise. Included in this practice is having teachers lead sessions as often as possible to support each other, using them as experts in their own craft. The second power is in giving and receiving instructional feedback. There are a variety of ways that teachers can receive feedback, both informally and formally. Walkthroughs are common in schools, and when used well, can help administrators gather critical information on what is actually happening in classes and can be very powerful for decision-making (Protheroe, 2009) not to mention the power they have in coaching teachers for improvements to practice. The powerful aspect of learning through coaching does not have to be done by a supervisor. If the school has well-developed teacher leaders, they can fulfill this role in a non-threatening structured manner. When teachers support one another and guide their own growth and development, they enjoy greater connections with the change efforts, with one another, and with the school goals. This is all about the quality levels of support that teachers need to produce their best results, which really does require feedback as often as possible based on real instructional practices in the classroom.

SUPPORT AND GROWTH THROUGH FEEDBACK

In a learning culture, walkthroughs are a great opportunity for administrators to see what's actually going on in the classroom. In a well-developed aligned system, the walkthrough specifically looks for elements of the instructional focus. In our literacy scenario that we outlined before, the walkthrough would specifically look for evidence of the PD within the lesson planning and instructional delivery. Just as the observer should make the "look-fors" well known to the teachers, the teachers should solicit feedback on specific practices that they are working to hone. If we truly want to assess how well a strategy is being implemented at its best, teachers should feel comfortable asking an administrator or coach for support, telling them what to look for and when they are doing a particular activity to get feedback on it. In addition, this process doesn't have to be evaluative either. In fact, it should always focus on strengths. The goal is to learn and master skills in a risk-taking environment where we all can offer clear and direct feedback to one another to improve practice. This type of feedback focuses on predetermined goals, championing strengths and growth, and building on the professional learning taking place. As one Gallup study found, feedback, focused on strengths, dramatically increases employee engagement and helps create and nurture a culture where the employees matter (Brim & Asplund, 2009).

Ultimately, this approach to feedback and growth flips how internal change normally occurs. It changes the one-size-fits-all method of PD and once-a-year feedback structures to include access to various levels and types of PD, opportunities to learn over time, and an ability to demonstrate learning in an environment where it's safe to try new ideas. This helps teachers reach a greater number of students through a focus on doing things better and differently than before. This level of engagement creates connection, which brings joy and fulfillment. Both of these feelings allow for creative ideas to flourish, and the result is passion.

LEADERSHIP: CHOOSING YOUR DIRECTION

The art of systems alignment through PD and feedback is in making sure that all of the moving parts flow together well and that everyone is accounted for and on board. Once the system is aligned and a shared understanding has been established, the team can move forward faster, and true gains can be achieved. Great school leaders realize that to develop a passionate staff, devoted to their own growth and development, they must be at the forefront of change. A learning culture is a place where everyone welcomes feedback because they are committed to their own growth. It's the leaders within the organization who champion the movement from a teaching culture to a learning culture, and the resulting relationships that ensue become stronger and deeper because of the important changes that we're making for ourselves and kids. When people can see and feel the results of their labor, when they produce something new, and when outcomes are tangible, they realize that the cycle of improvement is important for the soul. This is where passion palpates from the every corner. It takes leadership, regardless of its genesis, to effectively impact the classroom practices of today and transform the school culture of tomorrow. Everyone must be committed to learning for their own sake and for the sake of everyone else.

CHARTING THE DIFFERENCE

A learning culture, where teachers are actively involved in the process, procedures, and accountability, possesses a certain "look" and "feel" in schools. Yes, it accounts for the changes that must be made from the outside, but it also creatively blends what the school leaders know needs to be done. The changes include input from the classroom experts on how they can best be achieved. This triangulation of sources is powerful but it needs to be explicit. Consider two of the descriptions below, *dynamic* and *resilient* versus *passive* and *submissive*. Effective school leaders realize that staff members who take ownership of their learning and grow through feedback have a much greater chance at success. This helps foster their individual and collective persistence through change because it deepens their capacity for the work. An environment where the staff feel detached and uninvolved in their own learning process will experience high turnover and low morale.

The learning culture taps into the school's inherent love, passion, and commitment to young people by growing people in new and important ways. We offer language to distinguish the differences between learning cultures and teaching cultures to show that learning has to be authentic and intrinsic for people with a growth mindset. This means changing some of our current conditions and it means offering opportunities to fuel passion in the people.

Figure 1.1 The Difference Between a Learning Culture and a Teaching Culture

Learning Culture	*versus*	Teaching Culture
Dynamic		Passive
Motivated		Uninspired
Courageous		Fearful
Resilient		Submissive
Supportive		Compliant
Authentic		Unreliable
Intrinsic		Extrinsic
Growth		Fixed

FUELING PASSION THROUGH OPPORTUNITY

Instructional technology is one area where schools are experiencing rapid growth, which is very often driven by teachers. In many cases, instructional technology is pursued and desired by teachers who support and lead their own training, professional development, and experiential learning. Whether the PD is concentrated on the uniqueness and potential power of a device or an engaging assessment program, which might allow teachers to quickly check for student understanding, there is a level of ownership by teachers on how technology can and should be used in the classroom. In this regard, many teachers are taking ownership of their own learning and finding creative ways to reach all students. In response to this technological implementation wave, schools have designing full learning labs for teachers to experiment and try new devices and tools to successfully integrate the technology into their classroom. This type of PD and growth is not a one-and-done or full-day sit-and-get experience. It is an ongoing mastery of the tools and techniques that is rapidly changing the profession. It's a clear example, which can be found all over social media, of how teachers are fueling each other's passion for tech integration to leverage the greatest tools to maximize learning. It's a learning culture movement.

The amazing thing is that these tools are not in and of themselves making a difference regarding student achievement. Passionate educators are discovering creative ways to supplement their best practices to enhance their current high levels of instruction. The device itself may be unique but it's real value is that it enables teachers to tailor their instruction in a manner to deliver it effectively to meet students' needs, orchestrating new ways of content delivery and learning. Technological enhancements give the teacher more control and opportunity for all students to master the learning. Interestingly, despite how rapid technology changes, and how, at times, it is frustratingly unreliable, it is embraced by so many. Because the instructional technology movement is organic, igniting passion through curiosity that extinguishes fear, teachers' willingness to grow is authentic, intrinsic, and contagious. In many ways, this movement has brought the pursuit of teaching, and the joy of learning, back into the profession. It's not another series or a new standard; instead, instructional technology creates the need for learning and even the desire for feedback on its use. More than ever, when it comes to tech advancement in the classroom, teachers are collaborating, working together to solve this new problem, seeking their own professional learning, and soliciting feedback. What we're saying is that should be the norm with everything we do—better professional development and more feedback on practices. The good news is that the technology movement is a perfect example of how it can work to inspire passion.

A CULTURE OF JOY AND FULFILLMENT

In the right environment, not only will the desired learning and development take place, but entirely new possibilities for growth will occur. The key is that the culture has to create opportunities and allow for exploration and development. There's no better place for this than a classroom, which should always act as a laboratory where learning creates opportunities for both teachers and students.

CREATING A LEARNING CULTURE BY DESIGN: COMMITMENT AND DESIRE

The following are two primary ways to develop a learning culture fueled by passion:

1. *Build an environment **committed** to growing and learning.* Passionate educators, in the right situations, embrace the notion that learning is communal and that great ideas thrive and grow among thought leaders. Professional development can take on many forms, but one way we see this is in high-performing professional learning communities (PLCs). High-performing PLCs work within a cycle of development that seeks to understand where their students are performing, how they can best address the needs, and develop their own skills to do so. The growth is made faster through the sharing of best practices. Add in the administrator, and the PLC can be guided with current research and ideas, as well as support

with resources. This level of organic growth and change is completely different than the outside-in, initiative-driven culture that is found with much of the current educational reform. In a PLC-driven environment, there is a shared responsibility among everyone and the impact of the team approach becomes clear. At the heart of the decision-making process, the school personnel are viewed as authorities and supported as professionals. A common notion that we accept as gospel is that learning should be fun for students. We argue that fun is just as important and relevant in professional learning for the teachers. The goal is that professional learning is new, differentiated, provided by experts (internally and externally), and exciting.

2. *Build a space that* **desires** *feedback.* The learning culture, as veteran English teacher Ry Culver and assistant principal Justin Comegys explain, is truly about creating a space that is free for both teachers and students to develop and grow. These two educators push the instructional boundaries by creating demanding learning environments where the process of learning takes precedence over simply disseminating information. They believe that the classroom should be a space where teachers and students are encouraged to try new things within the scope and goals set by the school. This space doesn't stop inside classrooms. It grows throughout the building as a community of learners get support from colleagues and administrators to take risks and seek feedback. Culver and Comegys are examples to demonstrate that as the efforts grow, and greater needs and support are identified, the learning space goes beyond the classroom and is brought to the attention of people outside of the schoolhouse. This drives passion and success. The more we share, the more we grow, and that harnesses joy, which empowers teachers to own their own learning through development and feedback, and it creates new ideas for the betterment of children. (Check out @twoguysde for more.)

The great news is that we know about and we've learned from wonderful schools and systems that are achieving impressive results in environments that build one another up yet still have high levels of accountability. They are using a learning culture to speed up the growth process for everyone so that we can manage change while striving for excellence with everything we do. In the next chapter, you'll meet extraordinary people who exemplify these efforts through passionate leadership for teaching and learning.

A Framework for Growth Through Reflection

Think: What Did I Learn?

Plan: What Do I Need to Do?

Act: What Will I Begin Today?

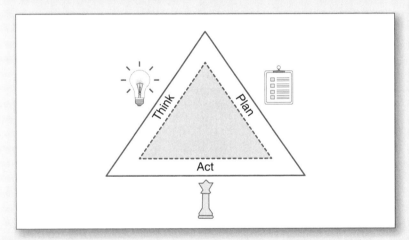

- Refer to Figure 1.1, *The Difference Between a Learning Culture and a Teaching Culture*. Using the descriptors, is your organization a learning culture or a teaching culture and what are some of the reasons as to why that may be? *Think*
- How will you shift your mindset to embrace learning and growing to be more effective in your current role? *Plan*

(Continued)

(Continued)

- What initial action steps do you need to take to design a learning culture in your organization? *Action*
  - o Identify your *greatest challenge* regarding the development of a culture committed to growing and learning.
  - o Identify your *greatest opportunities* regarding the development of a culture committed to growing and learning.
  - o Identify your *greatest challenge* regarding the development of a culture that desires feedback.
  - o Identify your *greatest opportunities* regarding the development of a culture that desires feedback.

Developing the Desire for Change to Grow Faster

"The world as we have created it is a process of our thinking. It cannot be changed without changing our thinking."

—Albert Einstein

SPEEDING UP THE PROCESS

Change is a common topic in educational literature. An enormous amount has been said and written about the need for change in schools, managing change in schools, and what it takes to make schools better through transformation (Alvy, 2017; Reeves, 2009; Whitaker, 2018). But we're adding a twist by calling for speed and precision. Schools need to leverage best practices to speed up the change process and identify what is necessary to grow and develop educators *faster* as leaders, learners, and teachers. We don't think common reform efforts and canned programs produce the results educators and others desire—although, doing something different is definitely better than doing nothing at all. The fact remains, simply doing the same things over and over again and expecting better results isn't the answer. Speeding up the change process to grow faster can be defined with two powerful and obvious but underutilized catalysts for change in schools: professional development (PD) and frequent feedback. You may be thinking, "Wait, these guys are going to tell me that we need to be doing PD and providing more feedback to each other? . . ." Yes, but let us redefine these practices so that you can see how they can help you grow faster when done effectively in a uniquely different way with passion at the center of each.

For change to be effective and for it to make a positive impact in schools, a critical need is a culture where everyone has a growth mindset. "When entire companies embrace a growth mindset, their employees report feeling far more empowered and committed; they receive far greater organizational support for collaboration and innovation" (Dweck, 2016). In schools, educators must believe that they can grow beyond their current skill set and they must be willing to engage in growth-oriented exercises. The keys to this culture are strong connections among colleagues, especially between the principal and the teachers, and a belief that everyone can and will grow. This reinforces the learning culture—a culture of growth, forged in care where strong relationships are vital for cycles of improvement to be sustained, and candid conversations, accepted as the norm. The benefits of strong relationships and clear communication is in how growth becomes systematic, which is needed for professional development to inform and improve professional practice and for feedback to serve as an instrument of change. Both are change agents for getting better at the job and representing to students that learning is an ongoing and lifelong process for everyone. When educators embody the values that they desire to see in their students, they become a beacon of learning for them.

The way to achieve this is through the relationships and support among the staff. One of the most prolific writers of leadership literature, John Maxwell (2010), identifies making connections with people as the key to success in any organization. He tells readers

> I'm convinced more than ever that good communication and leadership are all about connecting. If you can connect with others at every level—one-on-one, in groups, and with an audience—your relationships are stronger, your sense

of community improves, your ability to create teamwork increases, your influence increases, and your productivity skyrockets. (p. 3)

These connections serve as the bond necessary among people while growing and striving toward a common goal. Change is often personalized and can threaten people and environments, so a prerequisite for impactful professional learning experiences and transformative quality feedback is strong relationships. A meaningful connection with those you serve allows learning and growth to inspire and support change. These efforts, grounded in passion for student success, are what switch schools from being teaching centered to learning centered. Learning-centered schools have cultures where every person is poised to learn new and different ways to engage with students to improve the rate of success the school experiences. A learning culture coupled with a growth-oriented environment recognizes the need to do things better each and every day with the faith and belief that we'll be even stronger tomorrow. Schools that embrace that learning is an integral part of ongoing growth and development have a psychological advantage in that they yearn to get better and seek ways to do so. The advantage lies in the openness to change and the resulting speed at which we grow when everyone willingly works to better themselves and actually wants feedback to improve their practices. To truly realize a culture of growth, we must accept that "you never arrive once and for all, nor should you want to" (Fullan & Quinn, 2016, p. 2).

Two factors emerge in a culture where growth is a core value: (1) People look for and crave professional learning experiences outside of the typical PD offerings in schools, and (2) Everyone is driven by the feedback that they give and get from one another. In schools where these two things are the norm, growth-oriented change is also the norm, and passion is palpable. These factors are not complicated or even new, but somehow for many educators, professional development has gone sour and the idea of frequent visits to the classroom followed by feedback seems intimidating. We want to reverse these feelings by invigorating leaders with the ardor to ensure that these two important aspects of leading a school are front and center. We have to change our thinking if we want to change and improve our schools. When quality PD and feedback are at the forefront of growth and change, the entire staff will accept the concept that we all also need a personalized growth plan. We're going to go as far as saying that all of your people should want an improvement plan and no one should get hired without a growth-mindset background check. We're changing the language we typically use from "improvement plan" to "personalized growth plan," but essentially the point is the same—everyone needs to learn and grow, and that takes strategic planning. When we demonstrate our passion for growth and growing each other, we build bonds that permeate the culture. We begin to see professional learning as key to our personal improvements and feedback as a driver to help each other get better faster.

FEEDBACK FASTER: CREATING SYSTEMS OF IMPROVEMENT

Smerek (2018) reveals that organizations narrowly spend too much time on "exploitation" versus "exploration." He tells readers that organizations tend to exploit their products and practices for too long, making things more efficient but without looking for ways to innovate. On the contrary, there should be a balance whereby equal time is spent on exploring totally new opportunities.

> Exploration includes stepping out of the flow of experience, however momentarily, to generate new ways of thinking that can help you adapt for the long-term. It includes having a *learning-focus* where you share information, actively develop individuals, and promote curiosity. (p. 2)

To this end, learning organizations are a balance between doing what they already do well, just better, and finding new and innovative practices to hone and implement. Learning organizations are places where all are dedicated to their own development, where new ideas are encouraged, and where cycles of feedback are frequent, systematic, and aligned to the goals of the organization. This is precisely why we need to rethink how professional development is structured in schools. Typically, PD is provided at specific times throughout the year, usually in whole-day sessions. Common practice is that all teachers receive the same type and dosage no matter their years of experience, subject speciality, or expertise. Most PD providers are set up to deliver in this format because that's the way the school calendar is designed—a few days a year where students stay home so that teachers can develop professionally. But, most teachers will tell you that this model is broken, busted, and beat. While our most passionate people may grab nuggets of newness on these days, everyone else is bored to death, grading papers, and surfing the Internet on their phones while the facilitator drones on.

In fact, in many schools and organizations, professional development is something that is done *to* you, not *with* you, even though it's supposed to be *for* you. We've all heard people ask, "What are we doing this year for professional development?" The simple question implies that someone else planned the day and the people receiving the PD were not an integral part of the planning and development. We aim to flip this outdated model of learning so that PD is both an exploitation of what we need to do better and an exploration of what everyone can learn to do differently. It's a key factor in fueling a staff passionate about their growth and ultimately their students' achievement.

In this same vein, classrooms cannot function in isolation as silos where feedback regarding teaching and learning is infrequent and inadequate for learning to be the outcome. In many schools, feedback to teachers is about compliance with an evaluation system and not a growth-oriented experience. In learning cultures, the classroom is a lab where teachers strive to instruct to the best of their ability and enable students to push themselves to master material. As a result, feedback is welcomed, anticipated, and expected. Unless your teachers are driving into work welcoming and desiring quality feedback from visits to their classrooms by an administrator or coach, you're not quite to the point of a complete growth-oriented culture. We do believe our formula can get you there and inspire an intrinsic desire to be better. Consider first, revamping the way we think about and conduct professional learning.

Professional Development. As stated above, professional development in schools needs a makeover if people are going to be passionate about learning *with* and *from* one another. The biggest problem with most current approaches is that they are one-size-fits-all. In a time when personalized learning is a key feature of our planning for students, we must also create a personalized approach to PD for all staff. Bray and McClaskey (2017) tackle the topic of personalized learning for students with advice about having a shared vision and common beliefs; creating systems for learners to be independent, self-directed, and motivated; and initiating a culture where learners thrive. This is precisely the direction that we're going with professional development for our teachers.

The goal is for professional development to systematically grow the learner so it translates into improved practice in the classroom for greater student achievement. Unfortunately, this goal is not met when the models of professional development are unengaging, not differentiated, or implemented poorly. Joyce and Calhoun (2010) remind readers that "poor implementation can make any [professional development] model ineffective" (p. 3).

A great example is Michele Lind, principal of Cathedral Elementary in Bismarck, North Dakota. Michele has a pure desire to create systems of learning among her teachers through personalized professional development. As the school leader, she does things differently to make learning fun and relevant to her staff, so she planned a "book tasting." She uses a faculty meeting to introduce a bunch of books that teachers will choose from for a book study. "The objective," she says, is to "personalize the learning by allowing teachers to choose the book while also encouraging ongoing learning and improvement." She set the meeting up like a restaurant, and the teachers get to "taste" the books at the "dining" tables to choose one to read for a book discussion at the next early-out professional development day. We loved this idea because it differentiates professional learning, allows choice, and fits into the growth mindset that passionate people have and instill in others. Michele is a great example of how leaders can make learning fun for the staff while building a learning culture. This is especially fantastic work because it layers and differentiates professional learning for the teachers with a new idea for book study.

In addition, as educators, this type of PD, with its focus on reading to grow, models to our students that lifelong learning is critical and that the staff is committed to getting better for their sake.

Quality professional development has to be layered. As mentioned, the one-size-fits-all singular format that lacks differentiation, support, or choice is ineffective. We have to break the mold and look outside of our schools, outside of our typical conferences, and take professional learning to the next level if we want teachers, or any staff member, to be excited and passionate about improving. We have to not only flip the thinking from the staff passively accepting that this is something happening to them by a disconnected facilitator to a belief system that recognizes the value of improving and an understanding that the PD will be beneficial. This creates a love, a craving, and a desire to truly want to get better. Passionate schools are about extreme growth and that only comes when everyone is ready to learn new practices, share new ideas, and get involved in special programs at the district, state, and national level.

These stories are real and epitomize the passion we desire to cultivate in every organization. We're fortunate to receive permission to use real names and feature inspiring work. We want to introduce you to Dr. Raymond Theilacker, a modern day renaissance man, passionate educator, and wonderful friend. Ray taught for many years in New Jersey, Pennsylvania, and Delaware. He was an advocate for the profession, a union leader, and, in the purest sense, a lifelong learner. Without any interest in administration and long before programs of study at this level were designed for teacher leaders, he earned his doctorate in educational leadership from Wilmington University. Ray, an English teacher by trade, wrote his dissertation on improving students' writing skills through the use of poetry. He was an optimist who never gave up on an idea that might foster the development of the people around him. His pursuit to grow and his belief that others also desired and deserved more, is precisely why he was a perfect match for the Yale National Initiative (designed to strengthen teaching in public schools).

Providing Unique and Important Teacher Professional Development Opportunities

Dr. Raymond Theilacker, Director
Delaware Teachers' Institute
Newark, Delaware

Ray Theilacker was a public high school English teacher with over 35 years of service when he was introduced to the Yale National Initiative (YNI). He was invited to attend an annual summit in New Haven, and as someone who never turned down an opportunity to learn, he went. After his experience, he was so well entrenched in the belief that teachers needed this type of professional learning that he retired from teaching to create what is now the Delaware Teachers' Institute (DTI) at the University of Delaware, but that's not where the story begins.

As a well-respected teacher and leader, Ray was known for his desire to improve his own craft, and really, the art and science of teaching in general. With a note from his superintendent, who had a distinct curiosity in knowing more about the institute, Ray left for a two-week stay on Yale's campus to experience YNI firsthand. Maybe Ray knew from the beginning that this would turn out to be more of a calling than a summer program, but that didn't matter at the outset. Regardless, what was evident was the fit. YNI is a personalized experience, bringing together elements of cross-curricular planning, cross-grade-level thinking, curriculum unit design, and pure content expertise. Moreover, the approach establishes a collegiality between K–12 educators and university professors in a way that emulates professional learning communities at their best. Ray enjoyed the professionalism and what could be considered pampering that the teachers received as an integral aspect of the program. As someone who saw education as a regal profession, he realized the nobility in what Yale had to offer to teachers as both humans and learners.

His first summer was spent working arduously on a unit plan for his English classroom. The primary outcome for YNI participants is a curriculum unit, aligned to standards and informed by both the other seminar participants and a university professor, called the "seminar leader" so as to extinguish any hierarchy in the group. The improvements that each teacher makes to his or her unit plan are iterative and grounded in feedback from the seminar leader and other participants. So that's the program . . . participate in an initial meeting, attend for a two-week stay in New Haven to write a unit to teach the following year, and submit the unit to a bank of curriculum units, provided as an free online resource for teachers around the world. For Ray that was enough—great program, great people, great outcome. But that's not the whole story.

When Ray returned from YNI to teach his newly developed unit and to report back to the superintendent about what he had experienced, he was energized by what he had accomplished and the possible opportunity to return. He boasted of the way YNI is structured so that teacher leadership drives the initiative at its core. His excitement inspired the superintendent, and the prospect of sending even more teachers to YNI the following summer became a focal point for the district.

Ray recruited a few other teachers to attend the next summer. They all agreed that the program was one of the best professional experiences of their lives. And, the goal of the institute was achieved, teachers creating a world-class curriculum unit they would teach during the upcoming school year. In turn, the students would benefit from the time that the teachers spent planning lessons and activities— time that most teachers don't have in a regular school year to dedicate for what comes from YNI participation. Ray emerged as the leader, helping them to think about their units and reading their work for quality. He cared about the professional development as an experience for himself but more so he cared that his colleagues received the support they needed to be successful. The bonds were strong, and the initiative was making a difference in both teacher quality and in the relationships that were formed.

Ray realized something in the midst of writing a new unit to publish in the YNI bank of units that he now had available for his personal use as a teacher. He realized that the invitation and his ongoing participation with YNI was very special. YNI was a hub for other remote institutes, built after the YNI model in places around the country. He learned that some YNI participants became leaders of local institutes, connected to their own universities, and that the Yale leaders were interested in branching into his area, just as they had in so many other states and regions. Ray was up for the challenge.

(Continued)

(Continued)

The point of YNI is to reward teacher leaders for their participation in a local institute and build them up as leaders to sustain their institutes with new participants and strong partnerships. Every institute has a director who reports, in most cases, directly to the university president. Institutes are meant to build partnerships between school districts and their nearby universities to provide quality professional learning experiences for teachers. The beneficiaries are always students. When we strengthen teaching, we strengthen the whole community.

Fast forward, Ray built what is now the Delaware Teachers' Institute (DTI) at the University of Delaware. During the writing of this book, it is the largest and most prolific teachers' institute in the country (rivaled only by the good folks of Philadelphia who are doing similar work). He enlisted teacher leaders, like Barbara Prillaman, who championed the cause and made sure that superintendents were informed and committed while Ray built relationships with the university. More teachers participated in DTI each year with more and more support from university faculty. The result is a small group of passionate people committed to mastering their craft and who are making a major impact on professional learning in Delaware and beyond. The curriculum units are published for any teacher to use, and DTI is growing as you read these very words.

We're sad to say that Ray passed away, and for all his family, friends, and colleagues, it was way too soon. During his entire endeavor of breathing life into DTI and bringing it into the world, his own personal health was being challenged. He suffered from a heart attack and then cancer, which he battled not once or twice but several times before it took his life in July of 2018. Ray gave his best against the insidiousness of prostate cancer, skin cancer, and lymphoma, which ultimately made him too weak to treat. Ray lived his life with fervor and a belief that through education we all can become better, all the way up until his last breath. Imagine his strength, in constant assault by disease while building a program from the ground up. Anybody else might have simply given up. Not Ray. His death was a shock to the people who knew him because he literally had bounced back so many times before. A colleague and partner in the development of DTI, Barbara Prillaman, said of Ray that she took for granted that he would overcome the last diagnosis. She said, "That's just what he did; he got sick, he got treated, and kept moving." That's passion at its best, so passionate about teaching and learning and the growth of the profession to literally dedicate your life in service of it, despite the adversity that often meets our match. And it's our hope that through this book, the story of Dr. Raymond Theilacker, and the Delaware Teachers' Institute in affiliation with the Yale National Initiative, will never die. We dedicate this work to Ray and folks like him who can't be stopped in the development of programming that supports the profession. We leave you with 3 Key Takeaways before we take a look at the other element of true passion when it comes to the extreme growth mindset that we want to bring into every school.

3 Key Takeaways From Dr. Raymond Theilacker

1. *Seize opportunity.* Ray never turned away an opportunity to grow, and neither should you. Whenever a new or different opportunity arises, take advantage. Too often, we make excuses for ourselves that we're too busy or that we are already doing enough. Take action by finding a unique professional development opportunity this year and make it happen for yourself, the people who you lead, and the students in your school or classroom.

2. *Don't be afraid to be the first.* To be a true leader of a learning culture and to inspire others to grow faster, we often have to be the first. Ray initiated the conversation about building a local institute in Delaware. Pick something that might be new to your classroom, school, or district and introduce it to a group of people who can help you get your idea or initiative off the ground. Be the one who starts the program, initiates the conversation, or forms the committee. Don't wait!

(Continued)

(Continued)

3. *Spread the news.* Ray came back from YNI and he immediately went to work recruiting others to get involved. Next time you attend a great PD session or an inspiring conference, tell 10 people about it. Write down the names of the people in the margin of the note section of your booklet or handout, and be sure to tell others *why* it was so full of learning and inspiration. And, if you're not already doing so, get on Twitter to tweet the great things that are happening in your classroom and school. Do it now and join us using #passionateleadership. Grow your #PLN intentionally and spread the good word about professional learning, leading change, and growth.

Frequent Feedback. Schools with leaders who are speeding up the growth process for all educators are implementing systematic and frequent feedback mechanisms. Reeves (2016) calls feedback one of the seven "elements of effective leadership in education." He tells readers that feedback has to be fair, accurate, specific, and timely (p. 1). The problem is the over reliance of compulsory teacher evaluation systems that only call for infrequent usage, often with only one to three classroom touchpoints a year. Bambrick-Santoyo (2012) says that these once-a-year observation schedules are "foolish." He compares teachers to tennis players and posits that they will only improve rapidly through "frequent feedback and opportunities to practice." Instruction must be the focus for administrators and they must truly embrace the importance of being in the most important space in the building, the classroom. Provided administrators are fully maximizing their time, the only way for frequency of feedback to improve is to first cut back on the amount of time we stay in classrooms. The goal is to increase the number of visits to all classrooms by decreasing the visitation time. This allows for a stronger classroom presence along with more feedback to teachers, which increases the engagement between the adults, professional dialogue about practices, and passion for the work. Tammy Davis, of Central Elementary School in Artesia, New Mexico, told us that her walkthrough e-mails have really opened up lines of communication. She called her shorter more frequent visits "time-efficient and effective in providing springboards for meaningful understanding." Tammy explained that without the frequent visits, the evidence she was collecting about practices was insufficient to provide quality feedback or to make decisions about practice.

When administrators and coaches don't spend enough time in all classrooms to collect evidence and provide teachers with feedback to create meaningful dialogue, teachers don't benefit and administrators can't get good enough at it for the feedback to matter anyway. Worse yet, the once-a-year visit doesn't only limit the extent to which we can comment on a teacher's classroom environment and plan for that day, but limits the administrators ability to see the depth and complexity of the student experience in any given program of study. Instructional leaders have to visit the same classrooms often to see the nuances and subtleties between what it means to be a novice and a master teacher. Frequent visits over time provide a narrative of performance for the observer that might demonstrate the difference between group work and productive cooperative learning experiences or the variations in peer-to-peer interactions that result in strong relationships over time. Single visits don't reveal these distinctions and, as such, prevent leaders from commenting with authentic praise and criticism needed for teachers to refine their practices and respond with passion and purpose in our important profession.

This feedback cycle is critical if we want teachers and administrators to grow. Tepper and Flynn (2018) point out that although reflection is a critical element of teacher quality, "many times the teachers we coach require directive and guided feedback, as they are not ready or are unable to arrive at their own conclusions about the effectiveness of their lessons" (p. 96) without it. As instructional leaders, we have a moral obligation to our students to provide frequent and ongoing feedback to teachers. The instructional imperative is that administrators work tirelessly to improve all of their teachers. Our most passionate people, who we would clone if we could, are desperate for ways to grow. They crave feedback on their practices and they deserve it. Supporting and growing our best people only makes everyone better in a culture of learning.

This culture of frequent feedback is forged in passion with a growth mindset at the core. The environment is cultivated by a cycle of feedback and subsequent improvements to practice. When we see ourselves improving in a caring and supportive environment, we increase our passion for the work. Without feedback, teachers' growth is limited and the goals of the school are unreachable. With infrequent visits, leaders can't see the whole picture and risk giving uninformed guidance. This limited approach makes any commentary on lesson plans and interactions in the classroom seem foreign, scary, and intimidating. Simply put, sporadic and unsystematic critical feedback can create defensiveness. But a culture of frequent visits, deeper dives into classroom practices, and follow-up conversations about growth is supportive in ways that those of us who haven't worked in schools where this is the norm might not quite grasp how different it can be from the typical siloed approach to teaching. Let's take a look at a school leader who understands the power of this approach and who implemented it in more than one school, demonstrating the replicability of a culture of passion and the power of leadership, driven by doing what's right for kids.

Allow us to introduce you to Pete Hall, in case you don't know him already. Pete was a principal of a preK through 6 school in both Reno, Nevada, and Spokane, Washington, and he also served as a principal of a 7–8 middle school in Spokane. Pete has always had a relentless interest in his own growth as an educator as well as the growth of the teachers serving the students in the schools that he led. We interviewed Pete because of his feedback protocols that he implemented in all of the schools where he was principal. His philosophy and ability to create systems where everyone is expected to improve by getting frequent feedback faster than ever before is impressive. We hope you enjoy the story of his principalship as well as a few of his books, which we'll introduce after we tell you about what Pete did as a passionate leader.

Improving Systems for Providing Teachers With Feedback for Growth

Pete Hall, Speaker, Author, and Motivational Coach
Education Hall
Coeur d'Alene, Idaho

"I'm not a big fan of the status quo, and I say that because I'm a believer in continuous improvement." These are the words that Pete Hall lived by as he visited classrooms during his time as a principal. His story is unique, but it's not complicated. As a principal, Pete believed that the state-mandated minimum number of teacher observations was insufficient and would simply not work as a driving force for change. An obligation, as he put it, that is for simple compliance, which spurs only a regression toward the mean and rarely helps our teachers to improve their practices.

In both states where Pete Hall worked as principal, he always looked past the reliance on minimum requirements or even rubrics for levels of performance to a system that engages observers and teachers in the feedback cycle that is necessary to get better. His core sentiment is clear: "Rather than adhere only to the minimum requirements of the evaluation system, I opted to change that practice. Turn it on its ears." He knew each time he entered a classroom that his teachers needed thoughtful reminders, opportunities for dialogue, embedded professional development, coaching, and incredible levels of support if they wanted their students to reach new levels of success.

Pete's feedback protocol comes in the form of multiple layers of walkthroughs, each layer serving a different purpose, with the ultimate goal of teacher and school improvement through information gathering, feedback cycles, addressing problems of practice, taking a team solution-oriented approach, and formal evaluation. It looks something like this:

1. *Rounds.* These are quick visits to classrooms, never meant to be more than 30 to 45 seconds each, just to get a pulse of

(Continued)

(Continued)

the school and a gauge of how things are going in each classroom. They included a specific focus, previously decided upon by the team and communicated to the staff (instructional, climate, management, relationships).

2. *Walkthroughs.* These are 12 to 17 minutes each, geared at looking for what teachers have designated as their individual professional growth goals, the department goals, and the school focus for the year. Pete visits, watches, listens, and then engages in a feedback protocol, starting with an informal e-mail about what he saw, and then strategically following up with a face-to-face conversation after a few visits. The feedback was essential, and the follow-up coaching and support was a critical piece to continuous growth.

3. *Instructional rounds.* These are 30 minutes each, where Pete is joined by a team of teachers, instructional coaches, and other staff to visit classrooms to address a predefined problem of practice related to the individual and/or team area of focus. Pete took his team on "rounds" and then they debriefed together, identifying strengths, weaknesses, trends, and ideas that could impact changes in practice. This was all about learning and growing together to reinforce the culture of learning, not just a culture of teaching, among everyone to reach the goals of the school.

4. *Team meetings.* These are 45-minute meetings where Pete attended to observe and note how teachers worked together, engaged with one another, supported each other, and used their time, their space, their strengths, and their data wisely. Often called PLCs in schools today, Pete implemented these team practices before most schools were scheduled to discuss professional growth and student needs collectively.

5. *The formal evaluation process.* Pete didn't skip the state initiated formal process; it was just fifth on his list in the cycle of improvement. This included a preconference, a formal observation, and a postconference, with follow-up support when needed. The key here, more than anything, was the

two opportunities for professional dialogue about teaching, learning, and the state of affairs in the room he observed.

Pete's five-part system has two goals: (1) improve teachers' skills and abilities in the classroom, and (2) create a culture of reflective capacity to identify needs, address them intentionally, assess impact, and adapt as needed. The point is that the frequent feedback to teachers was systematic and purposeful, driven by a pure desire to get better.

Influenced by the publishings of John Dewey and Donald Schon, Pete Hall took an approach to passionate leadership that crushed the status quo. He wasn't just visiting classrooms with greater frequency or engaging in richer dialogue about classroom instruction—both critically important—he was intentionally addressing the needs of the people on the frontlines—the classroom teachers in front of our most important asset, the students.

Not only is Pete Hall a perfect example of a passionate leader, he demonstrates what it means to inspire passion. In our interview with Pete, he called his approach "a journey." He told us that the feedback cycle always ended with the teachers having most of the answers, only needing a guide for greater focus on analyzing what was working and what wasn't working. Each of the schools that Pete led saw gains in academic achievement and earned accolades in the process. Pete humbly gives all of his credit to the amazing staff that he had the privilege to lead at each of his schools and recognized their willingness to reflect and grow for the betterment of students. Pete currently serves as the executive director of Education Hall and president of Strive to Success Solutions and continues his passionate leadership approach to helping others through his writings, presentations, and consultation. We suggest his 2017 book called *Creating a Culture of Reflective Practice* written with Alisa Simeral. You can check out his list of works to inspire your passion and growth by going to www.educationhall.com.

Pete gives us an example of how we can increase our visits to classrooms, speeding up the process for growth in schools. Additionally, his layered feedback approach demonstrates how intentional his efforts were and how they were governed in a systematic process to ensure that the work actually made a difference.

3 Key Takeaways From Pete Hall

1. *Don't accept the status quo.* Leaders know how to crank things up to the next level. That's exactly what Pete did at each of the schools where he was principal. He recognized the status quo, and he added meaningful layers to it. He took the standard of acceptance and made his own standard of excellence. Right now, take a moment and think of something that you do in your classroom or school and add one layer to make it better. It might be a simple classroom strategy, a conversation you need to have with someone, or even the number of pages in this book that you plan to read before Sunday night. Take something that would otherwise be met with acceptance and give it one full crank more than normal.

2. *Informal feedback is critical.* Pete's story highlights the critical need for informal feedback. We have found that most systems of feedback lack authenticity and are sterile and formalized to the point where folks are in compliance mode just going through the motions. If that's true for you, or for anyone in your organization, add a genuine element of focus and a process for providing systematic informal feedback to teachers. Start by visiting every teacher twice per month to provide informal feedback on agreed upon teaching practices after each visit. Train yourself to build the visits into your week and commit yourself to being able to write the feedback during the 12- to 17-minute stay, hitting send on your feedback before you even leave the classroom.

3. *Culture is everything.* Pete described a culture where everyone had the desire to grow faster than ever before. A key takeaway is to always remember that it isn't *what* we do that matters but rather *how* we do it. Theodore Roosevelt is attributed with saying that "People don't care how much you know until they know how much you care," and nothing is truer than this when it comes to giving feedback and helping others to grow. Be intentional and explicit with how much you care about the people you intend to move to the next level. Tell someone today that you know how hard they're working and you appreciate their efforts to improve.

Just as Ray and others have shown that professional development is not a one-off experience, we need the aligned systems approach mentioned in Chapter 1 for growth and development if we're going to make significant and lasting changes in schools and districts. It's why our next section addresses the need to systematize professional development and feedback to create a culture of learning in schools.

SYSTEMATIZING PD AND FEEDBACK

These two powerful approaches, when used systematically, can have a significant impact on the school. To leverage them effectively both professional development experiences and cycles of feedback must be intentionally woven into the culture of our schools to create the right mindset around the practices and their outcomes. This is an attitudinal shift where the sentiment is "I crave learning experiences to help me grow" and "I require regular feedback on my practice to help me get better." In schools where PD is embraced, teachers are in search of new and different places to go and people with whom to connect. When feedback is embedded into the culture, they desire input and ideas to build into their daily work. This is flipped from "What are we doing for PD?" to "Here's what we should be doing for PD!" and flipped from "Why did I get another observation?" to "I'm excited about my walkthrough this week because I look forward to implementing the feedback I receive."

In cultures where professional learning is at the center of the organizational structure, the outcome is always a deeper connection to the work which creates passion, and it takes leadership to create a culture where a desire to change is a core value. This is a process of the thinking, which is that we come to work to learn *with* and *from* one another, and not simply to impart our knowledge on the students. In fact, everyone comes to school to learn, and we have to consider ourselves as classmates, altogether on a professional learning journey.

We organize professional learning and feedback into three segments for each person. This doesn't mean that a third of the attention is dedicated to each. Rather, it's meant to focus the growth experiences on only three areas for a school year so that the learning targets are clear and manageable. We tend to think of learning targets as only something for students, but the application can be precisely the same for teachers and leaders. Having clear goals and getting clear feedback are research-based best practices for teaching and learning, and we know them to be just as powerful with adults.

Figure 2.1 shows a sample of the three segments with an example of the focus within each area: (1) an area of focus for everyone, (2) an area of focus for your team or department, and (3) an area of focus just for you.

The key to success is that the targeted outcomes are clear ahead of time so that we know what we're working to accomplish. When the intended outcomes are in focus for the learner, deliberate practice toward the goal is possible. That means that we can then align professional learning experiences and feedback on practice to the focus for the school, department, and individual.

DEFINING THE OUTCOMES

One reason why Pete's work on professional learning experiences and feedback translated into practice is because it was done systematically. In addition, the practices were tailored and adhered to the essential work that needed to be accomplished. Everyone was clear on the targets and the scope of work. For learning to stick, outcomes need to be meaningful and tangible, and successful attainment of the goal should be clear. This also allows us to develop a culture of celebration and positivity, which is the focus of Part III.

Figure 2.1 Professional Learning Focus for Feedback

School Focus	Team/Department Focus	Personal Focus
Using collaborative structures in every lesson	Speaking in the target language for world language teachers	Creating stronger warm-up and closing activities for every period of instruction

In a learning culture, where the goal is to improve the students' experiences in the classroom, schools need research- and evidence-based strategies that they rely on for effectiveness. These strategies can come from a variety of sources, such as Hattie (2009) or Marzano (2003) about how students learn best and which teaching strategies yield the greatest results. The idea is to triangulate the teachers' learning targets with predefined outcomes that are aligned to the professional learning, all within the cycles of feedback (see Figure 2.2). We provide three examples of how this works in a school to demonstrate the power in defining these outcomes in the three critical areas we noted above.

Figure 2.2   Outcome-Based Focus Model

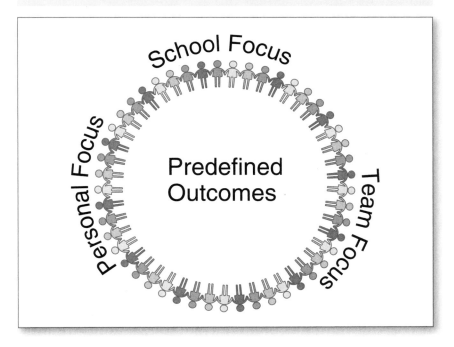

School Focus: Collaborative Structures. In the first example, the entire school focus is on collaborative structures and how well teachers organize cooperative learning groups and other opportunities for students to work together, such as using think-pair-share activities.

In this case, these structures should be executed with precision to ensure the strategy is fully leveraged and the students benefit from a well-organized and designed structure that fosters the benefits of peer-to-peer interactions. The professional learning throughout the year supports this initiative and administrative walkthroughs are designed to offer specific feedback regarding the school focus.

Team/Department Focus: Speaking in the Target Language. In the second example, we'll use a language acquisition classroom where students are learning to speak a new language. In this case, maybe we've determined that the teachers' time speaking in the target language is important for the entire department. To support this initiative and to ensure that students are learning the language, teachers know that this is a look-for during classroom visits. Again, the professional learning experiences for these teachers are targeted to this outcome—spending more time in the target language—and so is any peer, coach, or evaluator feedback.

Personal Focus: Warm-Up and Closing Activities. In our final example, the personal focus is on improving the learners' experience at the beginning and end of the period. We want to utilize warm-ups during lessons and better closing activities at the end for complete "bell-to-bell" instruction. As a result, much of the professional learning experiences that we provided for this individual staff member are tailored to high-leverage warm-ups and closing strategies that support her efforts to meet this goal. To support this endeavor, every classroom must be visited and followed by praise and recognition for meeting this new standard or some type of corrective feedback on how to implement the strategy differently. The culture is about learning and growing so the feedback has to be specific.

The sentiment here is not to ignore all other aspects of teaching and learning in our professional development experiences and documented feedback. Instead, it guides the work and recognizes the need for a meaningful deliberate focus that leads to success. We have to be laser focused for rapid growth to occur in a way that supports the needs of the school and the individuals within it. We have to include something for everyone, and for passion to become our purpose, we need clarity in how we can become better at what we do on a day-to-day basis.

SOMETHING FOR EVERYONE

Professional learning is never one-size-fits-all. It's the leader's role to inspire people to grow and get better, and that inspiration should manifest itself in exploration. Passionate educators are in search of new experiences to develop themselves and others, and these experiences are not always available in our schools and districts where the professional development is planned and prepared for us. We need to expand our view to discover local and national initiatives, bringing programming into our districts and sending folks out to every corner of God's good Earth. Passion for growing means that the culture of the school and the leadership team emphasize the importance of professional learning, self-reflection, feedback, and a growth mindset for every person in the organization. From the newly hired to the super seasoned, all staff members deserve to become masters of their craft and develop their skills. This requires a new lens on *how* and *when* professional growth opportunities occur. Later, in our section on celebrations, we'll say this again, but we call for staff meetings to be broken into thirds: one third celebration, one third information, and one third professional development. One powerful professional development method is to shine a spotlight on something that an individual within the school is doing well so that we harness her abilities to develop everyone while building our culture of collective efficacy. It is easy to highlight others, share success, and grow from one another when we're repeatedly in classrooms, giving praise and suggestions in the cycle of feedback. Everyone deserves quality professional development, tailored to the identified targets and needs that are evident by frequent visits to classrooms.

TECHNICAL TIP #1: EVERYONE GETS A PERSONAL GROWTH PLAN

Liz Ryan, *Forbes* contributor and CEO of Human Workplace, calls improvement plans "idiotic" and "outdated." She says that these plans tend to instill fear and stifle trust, and we agree. One primary reason is because improvement plans are only generally used for a few people who have poor performance. It's a no-brainer that this tool, which is rarely used, reserved only for people who lack skill, earns a negative connotation in the workplace. Consider, though, the intended outcomes of an improvement plan. It should, at its core, be a plan for someone to improve at work. For this reason, we want to debunk the notion that improvement is just for a few who are not performing well. We think everyone should desire to improve, which is why we want to reframe the thinking around improvement plans, and replace it with a "personal growth plan" (PGP) for everyone. To truly grow, we believe that each person should update his or her plan each school year to include the three following areas in a written plan:

1. *Self-reflection.* Online tools and educator evaluation programs abound, and we believe that no matter which way it's used, every teacher and school leader should include a self-assessment in an official PGP for every school. The assessment can be done a number of ways, but we think the reflection process should be ongoing. This means that everyone starts the year with a self-assessment and then the assessment gets updated at two or three other natural breaking points. An example of a natural breakpoint is during quarters when student grades are due, at the midpoint of the school year, maybe before a holiday break, or some other place where we naturally feel renewal during the school year. Hattie (2009) found that students' self-reported grades have a high effect size for learning and retention. We believe the same is true for teachers, where a culture of meta-cognitive practices is important as we reflect about our ideas, our thought processes, and our professional growth.

How-To: During the summer, develop a three-part form—a simple form with three boxes noted as *self-reflection, area of strength,* and *opportunity for growth* (see Figure 2.3). Then create a schedule for yourself, or for every teacher in the school, that reflects a beginning-of-the-year blocked time, middle-of-the-year blocked time, and end-of-year blocked time. These can coincide with other formal goal-setting conferences as needed. Begin the year with a self-reflection about your (and others') performance and contribution. Then follow up twice more in the school year. The key is that these "meetings" are scheduled ahead of time, using a real growth plan.

Figure 2.3 Three-Part Growth Plan

Time of Year	Self-Reflection	Area of Strength	Opportunity for Growth
Fall: Beginning			
Winter: Middle			
Spring: End			

2. *An area of strength.* Rath and Conchie (2009) unveil research done using interviews with over one million teams of people. They found three key things that make for good leaders: (a) Leaders ought to know their own strengths, (b) leaders must invest in the strengths of others, and (c) leaders need to enlist people with the right strengths to form a team. This applies directly to both classroom teachers, school leadership, and improvement planning. Written into the individual growth plan that we're calling for should be a strengths identification process. This allows for the teacher to build on her strengths in the classroom through focused professional learning activities for the year. It also allows the leader and other team members the ability to match certain strengths with other shortcomings for teaming, PLCs, committee work, and other important projects and initiatives. According to the research on strengths discovery, this approach can boost not only productivity but also happiness at work (McQuaid & Lawn, 2014).

How-To: It's not always the case that the right people are involved in our key initiatives, but it's critical to the sustainable success of any initiative that the right leader be at the helm. Make a list of your current projects and initiatives; next to the list, note the person who is leading the charge (see example in Figure 2.4). Then identify the quality of the fit and note if an adjustment or overall change should be made. Regarding future projects, assign the person to the project who has the greatest strength and influence over what you're trying to accomplish. Make your list today.

Figure 2.4 Initiative Alignment Chart

Project/Initiative	Lead Person	Quality of Fit	Possible Change
Blended Learning PD	Salome	Perfect	N/A
Parent Partnership Meetings	Joe	Pretty good. Lacks important English learner needs.	Sally or Jane. Possible co-lead with Joe. Brings enormous amount of expertise regarding special populations.

3. *An opportunity for growth.* Improvement plans are generally about critical areas of need, mostly deficiencies in performance. That's not what we're saying when we call for an opportunity for growth to be written into every educator's plan. We're talking about a genuine culture of learning within an authentic space that educators define as something that they want to know more about and get better at *or* something that they want to learn that's new to them altogether. The simplicity in this approach is that the learning experience can come from a teammate who can act as the resident expert or we can look for interesting resources to aid in the area of growth. The key aspect is the explicitness in documenting in the plan that we're all learners, looking to develop new skills and abilities.

How-To: Create a Growth Opportunity Plan (see Figure 2.5) on a spreadsheet (we suggest Google Sheets because of the sharing features). List all of the teaching staff in one column and then list any experience you can think of per person that will support their growth. Consider opportunities within the school, district, and state. Be as generous as possible with conferences and travel. When you invest in your people, the return is infinite, and the students are always the beneficiaries.

Figure 2.5 Growth Opportunity Plan

Teacher	Area of Growth	Growth Opportunity	Location
Salome	Instructional technology	Blended learning	Online webinar/ free
Sally	Working with high functioning autistic student	High functioning autism PD	Conference/out of state
T.J.			

This tip truly is about a culture of learning and not just a culture of teaching where people aren't feeling passion about their own growth or the growth of their students. People who are passionate about education take their own learning and the learning that transpires for others seriously. If we're sincere about growing the people who work in schools to meet the demands of every student, we need clear plans and structures within a support system to ensure that it happens. The old adage is that "a failure to plan is a plan to fail" and this directly speaks to school systems that don't develop plans to improve all educators.

TECHNICAL TIP #2: HIRE FOR A GROWTH MINDSET

We've presented evidence as to the importance of a learning culture where everyone has a personal growth plan and where everyone recognizes the need for feedback and desires to learn and grow. Passion exudes from people who desire growth experiences and who thrive on learning new things. The good news, and maybe the bad for some, is that certain individuals have a propensity for a growth-oriented disposition while others tend to be more fixed about their ability to learn and grow (Dweck, 2008). This reality reinforces the need for leaders to help people become more growth focused, but it also means that we should be on the lookout for growth-minded individuals and deliberately hire them. As an aside, schools of education within institutes of higher ed should be instilling a desire to grow into prospective educators as a prerequisite for working in schools. In any event, here are three practical ways that you can do your best to hire educators who already have a desire to grow:

1. *Add it to the job description.* Add something explicitly in the job description that notes to the applicant that *We're looking for people who have an extreme desire to learn and grow while on the job. We consider our culture to be one of continuous improvement, and we're only looking for people who want new professional learning experiences and frequent feedback on their practices. If you don't care to learn with us or accept our feedback, please do not apply.* When job descriptions are this vivid, you're bound to attract the most passionate people, and you'll keep others from applying.

2. *Ask for examples in the interview.* Ask for examples of recent professional development experiences and responses to feedback. Listen for professional learning that is taking place beyond what their current position requires. Listen also for ways that they've requested for and implemented feedback beyond the basics of their evaluation system. You'll quickly see the difference between passive and active learners.

3. *Use a scenario as a test.* Provide an example of a feedback situation where the candidate is getting critical and candid feedback on something that the observer would like to see done differently. Look for responses from people who implement the practice first and then reflect versus the opposite. This comes from *Practice Perfect* by Lemov, Woolway, and Yezzi (2012) who say that if we truly want to get better, we'll try new things and then think about how it went versus rebutting the new idea without practicing.

Hiring practices are always flawed, but we need to do a better job with specificity and scenarios. If we want to build cultures where passion spews from the inside out, we need to recruit people who can help us. These people ultimately develop a community necessary to support one another and celebrate the amazing opportunities we have with children. They also possess the skills to overcome many challenges that schools and students encounter. Once the internal school community is strong and focused on development, the entire educational community can be influenced. To have a lasting impact on our students and to achieve a world-class school system, everyone must be on board.

A Framework for Growth Through Reflection

Think: What Did I Learn?

Plan: What Do I Need to Do?

Act: What Will I Begin Today?

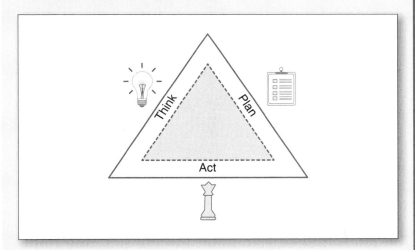

- What is one unique and important teacher professional development opportunity that you can offer to three deserving staff members this year? *Think*
- As you plan to develop a personal growth plan for yourself, what is one area where you need to grow? *Plan*
- What is the first step that you will take to create a culture that supports growth-oriented feedback? *Act*

Part II
Everyone Contributes
No Passengers Allowed

"There is no substitute for hard work."

—Thomas Edison

Our strength is developing a strong network of people within our educational communities, committed to ensuring that students succeed despite circumstance. Passionate educators and passionate people have an unwavering belief in children, and they work to support every child who walks through a schoolhouse door. They embrace the mantra that *Today I will work harder than yesterday because there isn't anything more important than now.* The challenges schools face are incredible and the burden to help our students succeed, at times, can seem insurmountable. Attending to all of their needs, many of which are beyond education, to support them and to equip them to be learning ready cannot simply fall on the school alone. We know that a child's academic success hinges on a teacher's ability to connect, instruct, motivate, and support. However, many people outside of the classroom walls, and even well beyond the school doors, can positively impact what happens within the classroom. Teachers and students need support, which should drive administrative decision-making and community outreach. If our goal is student achievement, then everyone within the educational community must be fully committed. This type of all-hands-on-deck mindset spreads the responsibility of our students' success to far more than the individuals working within the school buildings. It's the stories we tell about T. M., his parents, school, and a company, Wayman Fire Protection, that remind us about the power of connection and support that reinforce our work and remind us of how supporting students falls outside of the typical school day and that we all need to pull together.

Success Through A Passionate School Community
Every Student Is Everyone's Responsibility

T. M., Student/Employee
Wayman Fire Protection
Wilmington, Delaware

T. M. was diagnosed with ADHD at age 7, and by the third grade, he was coping with severe anxiety. He was attending counseling and therapy sessions, taking medications, and had an individual education program (IEP) to provide services at school, all intended to help T. M. be successful and reduce his extreme stress. Unfortunately, the medications were causing triggers and he started pulling his hair out of his head, arms, and legs, making him vulnerable to severe bullying. T. M. was at a point where he simply could no longer take it, and his parents felt like things were spiraling out of control. School, particularly middle school, was rough, and T. M. encountered other students who didn't treat him with respect, causing him to feel unsafe, unwelcomed, and, at times, threatened. How could this student with a promising bright future, supportive home, with a network of care from family, friends, and their church, be so stressed and filled with anxiety?

The key was that he needed continued love and support from the people he could trust. Fortunately, T. M. decided to attend a vocational-tech high school where he felt safe and discovered a welcoming niche in his technical drafting class. Additionally, his medications were finally regulating his ADHD symptoms and things were improving. His teacher was creative with making connections, he found like-minded friends, and he felt a sense of belonging in the class and the school where he attended. T. M.'s comeback and success was nothing short of remarkable and demonstrates what can be achieved in a caring, safe environment that raises the bar for our youth. A number of educators were involved with T. M.'s development along the way, and they supported him at school, but a great opportunity was made available beyond the school walls.

A new chance to show his growth as a person and demonstrate his skills came from a company which embraces the idea that educating children is the responsibility of the entire community. Alisha, the vice president, sought to bring him on board. Heavily involved with the school system through the ACE Mentoring Program—which is designed to provide real-life experiences in the world of architecture, construction management, engineering, and other disciplines through mentorship and coaching—Alisha knew T. M. could thrive at Wayman Fire Protection. She found the design department to be the perfect fit for this aspiring technical drafting student, and the rest is history. T. M. did well, his anxiety diminished through a newly thriving confidence in himself, and he finished school with success and earning scholarships. In the right hands, with the right support, T. M. was given the opportunity to utilize his skills in an environment that believed in him and supported him.

Not only does Wayman Fire Protection support students through mentorship and job opportunities, they participate in a unique outreach program through the Associated Builders and Contractors, Inc. of Delaware (ABC), designed to help students who don't have the necessary construction gear needed on the jobsite. This student assistance program helps students in the construction trades, recognizing that not every student has the means to buy the appropriate clothes, boots, or eyewear. This program creates meaningful connections with the school and local companies to help students overcome various obstacles that may prevent them from working and learning incredible hands-on field experience. Wayman Fire Protection champions their role in the community and within schools to support students and make a difference in the lives of kids like T. M. and others.

School is not always a friendly place for every student. T. M.'s experiences early on caused him to view school as a not-so-safe place to learn and grow. But through a network of support and commitment, all of that changed. Wayman Fire Protection's dedication to students and their learning is a terrific example of how stakeholders can take some responsibility for students and their success. Not only do they provide mentoring and cooperative employment positions, they are supporting their industry from within. They realize that when they give back to students and provide for the school, they are building the community, the economy, and ultimately their bench of ready-to-work employees. The great thing about this cycle is that when we have passion for what we do, through a supportive community network, we can inspire a whole new generation of workers. It's a wonderful thing.

The Wonder of a Work Ethic

"Only those who have learned the power of sincere and selfless contribution experience life's deepest joy: true fulfillment."

—Tony Robbins, *Awake the Giant Within*, 1992

EVERYONE CONTRIBUTES

There is a general belief held by many people around the world that recognizes a strong work ethic as important. This belief drives our behavior and our attitude about work, and it supports perseverance as a critical attribute to possess. We see inspirational commercials, we read about amazing feats in newspapers and magazines, and we honor people who have great accomplishments through ceremonies, events, and even through major film productions. We gravitate toward these great people and what they've done because they are inspiring, and they give us hope that anything is possible. One of the most obvious spaces where we see work ethic touted is among athletes. We've heard about incredible stories of tremendous athletes and the sacrifices they've made to become the best. Whether we look at the long hours that Larry Bird spent shooting free throws in his driveway in French Lick, the persistence and determination of Michelle Wie who qualified for the USGA amateur championship at the age of ten, or the incomparable drive of the great San Francisco Forty-Niners' receiver Jerry Rice, hard work and an undeterred focus is a clearly heralded and acclaimed characteristic to embody in some facets of our culture. These stories demonstrate that to be great, to be the best, you have to work hard. In fact, you must work harder than everyone else and go beyond what is expected to get the job done. Even Principal EL's incredibly gifted and talented buddy, Will Smith (2009), stated in an interview the only thing that makes him different is that he is not "afraid to die on a treadmill." Essentially, he will not be out worked. This desire to achieve, to push to new limits, is impressive and reveals that having a strong work ethic can pay off in wonders, leading to unparalleled success.

Unfortunately, this notion that a strong work ethic and that hard work can lead to greatness is not universally accepted within every pursuit. It appears to be situational and isolated to certain careers with higher rewards that culminate in fame and money, such as movies and sports, making these professions especially revered by young people. Somehow, working hard and persevering academically are viewed differently than those same characteristics within an athletic pursuit. In education, the idea of hard work tends to shift from pushing yourself harder to needing to do more work, which isn't viewed the way it is in basketball. Worse yet, students who work hard in school are either considered of a weaker caliber because they need to do so or they're named nerds and geeks for digging in deeper to their studies. Labels come quickly and from many sources. For some students, who have to or choose to work hard to study and learn, their efforts are neither glamorized nor championed. Their qualities are not viewed with strength, particularly for those students who struggle academically and need to put in extra time and effort to realize gains. In fact, if a student labors to learn, he is often viewed as not smart by himself and his peers. There exists an odd contradiction between developing yourself athletically and developing yourself academically. Of course, this doesn't stand true for a few students who excel academically, conquering difficult labs and impossible equations with a circle of support. These pupils are almost always found to have people in their lives who believe in academic achievement and who view education as the opportunity for greater success in the future. But, even these students are not generally viewed as developing themselves, but rather capitalizing on inherent strengths, talents, abilities, and God-given intelligence. For whatever reason, in our culture today, cultivating physical ability is viewed differently than academic ability, and we're proposing that this must change.

This generally diminished outlook on working hard academically limits students desire to persevere. In the minds of struggling students, schools quickly turn from a place to learn and grow into a place where their shortcomings and weaknesses are highlighted. Rather than embracing a growth mindset, students end up thinking that their situation is fixed, dismissing the idea that "everyone can grow through application and experience" (Dweck, 2008). This is what Duckworth (2016) describes as the "grit" that students need to push past the thought that their current situation is their ultimate lot in life. As a result, they don't believe in themselves, they tend not to believe in their teachers, and they see the system as something that has failed them. Yet, the research is clear on how students can succeed, regardless of the obstacles they face. Take, for example, the work of Albert Bandura (1994), inventor of the critical notion of self-efficacy, who describes how our beliefs about our abilities produce levels of performance that influence the actual events in our lives. Coupled with the more recent research conducted by Dweck (2008) and Duckworth (2016), and we get clear indications that students need to persevere and believe in their individual capabilities to learn in school and beyond. This work reinforces what Rosenthal and Jacobsen (1968) discovered in the Pygmalion classroom in how teachers' expectations influence student achievement, only to be further supported by Hattie's (2009) research on "teacher estimates of student achievement," producing a massive effect size of 1.29 on learning outcomes. This all reveals that for students to succeed, their own attitude and belief in themselves is critical, and the environment that they learn in is vital. They need a strong sense of self-efficacy as learners and they need people around them, including teachers and leaders, who believe that their contributions are worth every ounce of the work it takes to produce them. Blend this with strong support from the community and a "we must all contribute attitude," and the result is precisely what is necessary for greater student success.

EVERYONE MEANS EVERYONE

To create this reality, students need to shift their belief system about themselves academically, their values regarding the importance of learning, and their overall belief in the educational system. To achieve this end, every adult must represent the school system by demonstrating a work ethic through their attitudes and actions. The way to support this view of learning is through an educational community where everyone embraces the tremendous workload and reinforces a culture within schools that supports all students by recognizing and rewarding the learning process. For students to be successful, the school must have a "no passengers" allowed mentality, an attitude that everyone within the school, and those representing the school community, acknowledge and fulfill their individual yet critical role in supporting student success. This expectation reinforces how everyone must work together within the system to support the various parts designed as pillars for student achievement. Every person has a load to carry and a responsibility to shoulder the burden of their portion of the weight in making gains and pushing forward. A few cannot do the work of the many in building passionate schools that embolden children and the communities in which they live.

In addition to the critical notion we've outlined, a change in thinking about the work we do, there comes a realization that the wonder of a work ethic is truly an action that we all take, both physical and mental actions, whereby everyone contributes, nurtures, and cultivates a new environment that builds students up and inspires them to want to learn despite their circumstances. One district embarking on this work is the Colonial School District in Wilmington, Delaware. The superintendent, Dusty Blakey, established the *Power of We*, a vision emphasizing the collective impact of our work, from the teacher to the custodian, where we all make contributions to student success. The organization recognizes how each individual's efforts, regardless of her role, translates to success in the classroom, acknowledging that "collectively, we can move mountains, individually it takes forever to get to where we need to go." The attitude of *WE* is a passion-driven culture, permeating the entire district, which builds the foundation that student success is the responsibility of the entire school community. As a result, hard work, determination, and perseverance are reinforced regardless of the current academic situation of any given student. The narrative around student performance focuses on effort, applied study, providing supports, and being available so that every student has a level playing field through equity of access to quality programs. It's a culture of high expectations, strong methods for supporting one another, varied opportunities based on needs, and increased access for all students. And it is only possible because everyone reinforces the value of the learning process in a culture where passengers simply are not permitted.

These successful school cultures, with evidence from places like Colonial, recognize that learning is challenging and at times will require long hours in the classroom for teachers and several hours studying for students. The effort that it takes has to be supported and praised through a strong belief that all students can grow and learn. In essence, the school environment builds a hero's culture around everyone who is going above and beyond to succeed. The hero is not just the athletic superstar we see on TV, but the student who stays after school and perseveres, the teacher who goes above and beyond to help students learn, the administrators offering support from every angle, and all the school staff who see to it that their particular piece of the puzzle is completed with perfection. Passion-driven cultures build successful school environments because all within the school community understands the significance and importance of their roles and responsibilities, and they take ownership and pride in their contribution to student learning. Simply put, they strive to break the cycle of failure, embrace an "I believe" mentality, empower students, and represent families and the community with heart and hard work.

BREAK THE CYCLE OF FAILURE

Disrupting and ultimately breaking repeated cycles of poor performance and failure requires a group of skilled, committed, and passionate educators who possess the ability to successfully do four things: (1) They must have clarity on the areas of greatest need. (2) They must identify and differentiate between leading causes and enabling contributors. (3) They must possess the ability to harness the power of available and needed resources. (4) They must mobilize the school community to support necessary efforts. Each area is fundamentally important for sustainable success. Breaking the cycle is not easily done and requires a tremendous work ethic from every individual. The first step requires a raw authentic view of the current situation, to know and understand the areas of need. Too often, schools only have a partial view of the problem, relying only on common metrics and readily available sources of data. Using data to tell the whole story, and creating an accurate depiction of what is and what is not working, is critical to coming to an agreement and understanding about what the focus should be. The key is viewing data as a series of clues that should lead to more questions, more digging, and clearer answers. These uncompromising data-digs also require a willingness to face the harsh realities in many schools. Issues, especially those that are not easily resolved, are often complex and multilayered. Schools need to untangle the web of issues to uncover the root of the problem. Common issues such as a lack of parental support, low teacher morale, low student achievement, sporadic teacher attendance, high discipline referrals, and high teacher and administrative turnover are often symptoms of other deeper concerns, and are usually interconnected through a cause-and-effect relationship.

Although these are common situations that plague many schools, the approach to fixing them should always be unique to the system. Each school is different, which means that each school requires a prescriptive approach. Consider poor performance on the state accountability assessment at Simpson Elementary, as a fictitious example. Over the last several years, Simpson's test scores have been below the state standard. The school administrators and teachers know that the third-grade test scores need to improve, but their findings are fixed to surface-level inquiries; they don't dig deep enough into the data to gain clarity on what the real causes are, resulting in early treatments focusing on the problem incorrectly. In this instance, schools like Simpson very often review curriculum, instructional strategies, and other academic interventions to improve test scores.

On the surface, this makes sense, but let's say that in this case a deeper dive into the student outcomes data reveal that the cohort of students who actually start in kindergarten in the district are performing at grade level or above on the state assessment by third grade. As such, the data reveal that students who enter the system after kindergarten are the ones underperforming in subsequent tested years, and since the school accepts close to forty new students a year, the overall performance level is low on the aggregate. The low test scores are actually a result of students who enter the system late; they are not taught within the system the entire time. Knowing this information requires a totally different approach to fixing the problem. The school may establish an induction program, essentially a grade-level program to ensure students don't simply enter into a new class without the proper supports. A quick assessment can easily reveal deficiencies that can be addressed in a variety of creative ways by the school. This results in something far different than curriculum review or implementing interventions for every student.

There is no doubt that this process of data mining is challenging and requires an incredible desire to get to the heart of the issue. However, once schools have clarity by exhausting the data reviews, they are prepared to identify and set realistic goals, establish the appropriate next steps to accomplish them, and begin mobilizing forces to achieve the goals. Great schools, ones that defy the odds and experience success, start by first identifying their current reality, which allows them to uncover the leading causes and enabling contributors, which provides key insight into issues that might not otherwise get discovered. Once they have accurately diagnosed the problems, they must judiciously decide on the most critical areas of focus. This is important because the first steps to solving the issues must be manageable. Knowing the causes and contributors to critical problems empowers schools to apply the appropriate remedy, but it takes really hard work and a keen willingness to push past the surface.

This level of clarity ensures that the next steps will accurately treat the cause and move the school in the direction it needs to go to achieve its vision. Any approach to addressing and fixing schoolwide issues necessary to break the cycle of failure must be scalable and limited enough in scope for two predominant reasons. One, resources, both human and capital, are finite, so calculating the most important and effective steps necessary to achieve the goals is vital. The list of required changes and initiatives should be limited so that the approach is not only realistic, but that it can be supported with available resources on day one and pervasively for everyone. The goal is to make substantial gains in student achievement through needed programs, people, and resources that are sustainable. Two, schools, especially those who are underperforming, are usually already suffering from initiative fatigue. If a school is experiencing high teacher turnover, the last thing the administration can afford to do is to layer on a bunch of initiatives one after the other, which will only prompt the remaining teachers to update their resumes. The general tendency among administrators is that the greater the need for change, the more sizable and visible the better. The opposite is true, and albeit counterintuitive, focused hard work is the name of the game. In fact, because a school may need serious interventions and sweeping changes, the accuracy of the interventions and the fidelity of implementation is more important than the amount.

The last part of breaking the cycle is mobilization. Clarity on the issue and a realistic and well-developed plan is not worth much if it doesn't affect change. Inputs are great, but outcomes are what we need to measure. One great way to have a greater impact is to mobilize the whole school community. Students need everyone from the local legislators to the nearby businesses to know and understand what the school is trying to achieve. If we as a community understand and support what our local school is trying to accomplish then the chances of success are much higher. The school must function as one of the primary responsibilities of the community and not simply an entity within it. This should not be translated as increased oversight or the need for additional policies but more as a resource and reinforcement for the school. Simple examples, such as local community centers offering parents and students support seminars for dealing with at-risk behaviors or even the local technology store from the mall offering parental workshops on how to manage devices using parental controls, are powerful and comforting. The possibilities are endless but the intent is the same—the goals of the school are known by key stakeholders throughout the community and the school has the ability to rely on, lean on, and mobilize the community to be successful. Too many schools work in isolation, and the more problems they have, the lonelier they get. We have to break the cycle, and it takes skill and will. It's the reason we're writing this book, to demonstrate the power of combining the technical expertise needed with the hard work to make a difference.

All four components are critical to break the cycle of failure. In addition, there are key drivers that must be in place to support and sustain the determination to keep moving forward. Elements that blend the scientific aspects of this work with the emotional side, the courage needed, and the sheer drive to win. The next critical piece regarding full contribution and a culture of hard work is rooted in the profound desire among the adults to create an environment where all students can achieve success. It harnesses all of the efforts into a singular unified *I believe* attitude with no passengers allowed.

EMBRACE AN I BELIEVE ATTITUDE

The culture of the school must function through an "*I Believe in All Students*" notion to enable both the adults and the students to push beyond common limitations and self-imposed ceilings. Operating on the premise that all students can succeed creates a different mind-set among everyone. This seems like a simple idea, but it requires decision-makers to always use student success as the backdrop. Educators enter the profession with a desire to help children learn and grow to truly make a difference in the world. One of the greatest rewards in education is that we can directly experience the impact we make on students. So many professions operate with an abstract understanding and belief that what they are doing is beneficial for society, but educators actually experience firsthand each student's learning outcomes and personal development. As a service-based profession, one can actually see the results of our devotion to students and our commitment to perfecting the craft. However, this great benefit also comes with the stark reality of all the struggles and complications that can derail student achievement. Along with all of the joys and accomplishments, both large and small, there are also many struggles and heartbreaks. As one student succeeds in any given endeavor, there are several others who don't. Educating children is riddled with challenges that can strain even the strongest of school systems. Students aren't simply empty glasses that we hold under a faucet to be filled with knowledge. The truth is that they walk through the schoolhouse doors carrying far more than books and pencils. Many are saddled with unthinkable burdens and issues that prevent them from focusing on daily tasks and lessons. In the United States alone there are over 1.26 million homeless students, those without a permanent nighttime residence, according to the National Center for Education Statistics (2015). While so many are equipped for the challenges of the school day, many simply are not. Knowing all of the challenges students face leaves schools with the obligation to provide more than just a place of learning.

The goal is to see beyond the daily trials and maintain a positive perspective, fueled by passion. There's a need for a belief that underpins and pushes everyone to work harder every day, to embrace the current realities of educating students, and to build a strong foundation and network. We must avoid being overwhelmed by the work at hand or beaten down by our own previous failures. This outlook doesn't ignore all of the complications, issues, and realities that may be holding students back from reaching new heights, but it maintains a disposition that anything can be achieved if we all believe. This belief serves as a beacon of hope, offering promise to those striving for students to succeed, and it speaks to all students that learning is possible for you. As principal, Joe recalls a time when his student advisor, who handled the majority of discipline at his school, returned from the local thrift store with a bag of clothes in his hands for students to wear in their vocational classes. Since many of the classrooms were equipped with industrial equipment, only certain clothes were necessary or appropriate. Shop safety was a real concern and when students weren't dressed correctly; they couldn't participate due to the potential hazards. Not being able to participate typically led to additional problems, well beyond not getting a grade for the day.

Unfortunately, very often these were the same students who also found themselves late to school, cutting class, or being defiant. Rather than simply dealing with the situation from a disciplinarian viewpoint, repeatedly assigning detentions, Joe's advisor sought to solve the problem. The advisor decided to buy appropriate career-area clothing. They washed the clothes at the school, and if a student was "unprepared" for class, the tech teachers knew how to fix the problem with a solution that put the student back in the most important place in the school—the classroom. The reality was that for a few of the students just arriving to school every day was a struggle, let alone having the right clothes available, picked out, and prepared to wear. Rather than asking for help, they suffered the consequences and then acted out when they weren't engaged. The most rewarding discovery was that the students genuinely appreciated the clothes, typically jeans and boots, because it meant that they could learn their trade. Many didn't want to miss class; they just didn't have the means or the ability to advocate for themselves. Instead of punishing them for circumstances outside of their control, they needed the adults to advocate for them. This transformed the thinking from a mindset that assumed that students who came unprepared did so because they didn't care to a new framing around believing something altogether different about the learners who, indeed, showed up but who weren't ready. Instead, the adults shifted to solving problems, demonstrating care, and building incredible relationships that grounded in working hard for student success and a love for every student. For the students, not having the right clothes was just another reminder of how school and life were stacked against them, but it took a group of committed, caring, and passionate educators who believed the real lesson to be learned was in the classroom not in the detention room.

This mindset requires committed adults who believe in students and who are not swayed or deterred by circumstances. They are driven with a passion and zest that is contagious. This may seem naive or even Pollyanna; we've heard from some who consider it to be an unrealistic approach to this work. However, we maintain that it's just the opposite. It's a recognition that attitude and effort must be attended to with fervor and zeal and the way to do that is by recognizing the utter importance of the hard work it takes to educate every student. When everyone is committed, focused on common goals, and willing to support and motivate one another, morale will be high. This community of support is what keeps people motivated and helps maintain the right perspective, which is a culture that embraces the notion that *I believe, we believe*. We all need passionate leadership to get us there.

LEADERSHIP: CHOOSING YOUR DIRECTION

Although many educators and school systems aren't always fully equipped to meet the difficult issues students are facing. Successful schools recognize that each student is unique, with a variety of needs, which require professionals fully devoted to student success, as well as their own professional growth and well-being. This commitment is best forged in a high morale environment, committed to solutions and backed by a true sense of community. There are drastic differences in taking a communal approach versus schools that lack support and operate in isolation. We heard from one school leader who described her district as thirty-seven schools operating within a system versus a school system of thirty-seven schools. When we consider a true communal devotion to students, the result spills all the way into the power of the classroom and how that space transforms students' lives. It's a principled approach that recognizes that everything we do, regardless of the pressures heaped upon us, is designed for students to be successful. When everyone contributes with great effort, we uncover creative ways to solve common but difficult problems. This is a choice, often made by leaders, to chart a new course with new direction for classrooms, schools, and districts. It takes trust, love, and elbow grease—all of which are free resources. When we miss the free throw, we cannot resort to blaming the fans or admonishing our own skills, we simply need to show up before and after practice to dedicate what it takes to make the next one.

CHARTING THE DIFFERENCE

The chart below details the difference between schools that embrace a communal approach where everyone contributes and an isolated approach that allows for passengers. As a result of the communal descriptions, the success of students becomes the responsibility of everyone within a culture that supports the simplest of contributions and the smallest of efforts. This is a departure from isolated thinking, focusing on the small ways in which we build a community, which becomes the foundation and the momentum to achieve great success. It's a systems approach to bringing all the moving parts into alignment. Our collective efforts, not our individual contributions, creates a glue that holds everyone together, championing one another's efforts, sharing ideas, and taking responsibility for every student, every day. There's something sticky and attractive to being *cooperative* and *energized* versus being *disjointed* and *tired*. This communal way of schooling is created by leaders who value the work ethic required to start new initiatives, manage change, and provide ample opportunities for students, even beyond the school day. But it's the only way we can break the cycle of failure to realize success in our school systems.

Take, for example, *united* versus *divided* when it comes to after school programs. The *united* approach means that teachers are working together to offer programs that meet the needs of all students, before, during, and after school, supported by the system with resources, buses, and community leaders. The *divided* path leads to very few people staying past the final bell because the air conditioner shuts off, leaving the parking lot empty and students at home during a time when their parents haven't returned yet from work. *Divided* means that we all teach our subjects, doors shut, and not much else. Yes, there are individuals in poor performing systems who are making a difference, but a systems approach to working together actually lightens the load for everyone. If we all lift, our power is much greater than if only a few are doing the lifting.

Figure 3.1 The Difference Between a Communal Effort and an Isolated Effort

Communal	*versus*	Isolated
United		Divided
Collective		Uncoordinated
Cooperative		Disjointed
Accepting		Judged
Shared		Excluded
Reciprocal		Detached
Complimentary		Criticized
Energized		Tired

Of course, there are many factors that contribute to a school's success. Yes, many realities exist that are out of the school's control, such as tough socioeconomic conditions that can tear at the supporting structures because of the desperate living conditions from which our students come. However, a school operating in a supportive community, that is committed to creating and achieving success, has a much better chance than a school operating in seclusion. Through communal efforts and support, schools are far more equipped to not only teach but empower students and connect the adults who are stepping up to take on the challenge of a new day.

EMPOWER STUDENT OWNERSHIP BY CREATING NEW OPPORTUNITIES

A community of adults devoted to students is only one part of the equation. When parents, teachers, and local leaders come together, bringing contributions from every angle, the result is tremendously different than when schools are left to their own accord. But, students need to have a stake in the game as well. That's not to say that we rely on them to bring it. We have to instill it in them through a commitment to empowering each and every student. Passionate schools pinpoint that there are two things within our immediate control—our attitude and our determination. Effective school leaders appreciate this, and they capitalize on both to help students succeed. Over the last several years, there has been a tremendous push in schools to acknowledge the various needs of students from diverse communities, backgrounds, and situations. The one constant reality is that any student, at any time, may be facing challenges and feeling desperate, regardless of her outward appearance or perceived circumstance. As a result, many school systems have worked hard to ensure equity and access for all students. Enormous efforts and resources are mobilized to support this important work, and it's noted that it take courageous leaders to put the resources in place (Blankstein, Noguera, & Kelly, 2015). The report from America's Promise Alliance (2018) details "promising practices" within states that are implementing specific actions to ensure these equity goals become a reality. One example is Oregon's Office of Equity, Diversity, and Inclusion to ensure civil rights and "promote" equity. In addition to equity and access, valuing diversity is embedded within this area of focus, including great efforts regarding the social and emotional learning and support that students need. Whether this work is supported financially, or policies are established for greater awareness and accountability, the people doing the work are determined to help students succeed.

All of this work is done for good reason. Systems are critical, educators need to be equipped, and the allocation of resources must be aligned to the needs of the students. Furthermore, educators, at all levels, must be keenly aware of the gaps that exist between various groups of students, the skills necessary to meet the demands, and the opportunities and structures that students need to achieve results. This work only supports the *I Believe* attitude and the determination that marks the work ethic that it takes to perform at the highest level. The next phase, though, of this incredibly important work goes beyond the systems and cultures to the people who work within them and their direct empowerment of the students. There is no doubt that students need educators committed to this work to guarantee every student has access to a diverse, rigorous curriculum, within an educational community cognizant of the power of creating a successful culture. The staff, though, is only one side of the equation. Too often the programs, policies, professional development, and training is designed for the adults with the belief that it will positively impact the students. The belief is that a better-equipped teacher or leader will better equip the students. That notion works but only to an extent; it is reminiscent of the old adage that you "give a man a fish, you feed him for a day; if you teach a man to fish, you feed him for a lifetime."

The potential flaw is that all of these efforts may provide better opportunities but don't explicitly teach the students the fundamental principles of success. Essentially, what students need are specific skills that empower them and will make them learning ready, equipped with meaningful life skills. School efforts to create the right environment must balance a solid core curriculum with extracurricular activities that are designed to do more than just support reading and math. Academic opportunities alone aren't sufficient to empower students or teach them the skills necessary for life beyond high school. We fully recognize the system is overburdened with mandates and policies that restrict curriculum offerings and course-work, which is why schools must creatively find ways to teach and reach students outside of the general curriculum. We've all heard the conjecture and regular rhetoric about students who are passing through the system, lacking the necessary hard and soft skills after graduation. We broaden that term to "life skills" to cast a wider net to capture the skills necessary for the workplace and every other aspect of life. A recent report from the U.S. Chamber of Commerce (2017), acknowledged that despite "graduation rates reaching all-time highs, a growing number of employers across industries are reporting that job applicants lack the basic skills needed to succeed in the workforce" (p. 3). This is expressly the reason why we're call-ing for new, different, and creative outlets for students that go beyond the regular school day and often well into the evening. We're talking about unique programs, which we'll say more about in Chapter 4, and extra-curriculars, which comes up again in Chapter 6.

Interestingly, these types of studies focus on students who enter the workforce and who obviously had the academic status and requirements to do so. Imagine all of the other students who lack these hard and soft skills, which is why we believe students need to develop critical life skills to effectively use the hard skills we so desper-ately want to teach. In order to accomplish this aspect of teaching and developing students, schools must infuse a system that requires students to take ownership of four critical areas: (1) They must own themselves. (2) They must own their learning. (3) They must own their situation. (4) They must own their future. It's not dysfunctional for adults to take responsibility for student learning, but without equipping students with explicit skills that go beyond the 3Rs, it is arguably irresponsible. And the schools that are doing well with this are implementing programs that are far from traditional, which we'll demonstrate further in the next chapter. First, let's unpack the four critical areas of ownership.

The critical first step is to empower students to recognize who they are and to be comfortable with themselves and others. In other words, they need to own themselves. This approach blends the profes-sional development that teachers receive on the topics of diversity and mindset with actually teaching students to have grit and a per-sonal belief system about hard work. We started this chapter with students who may struggle with learning new concepts and finding school difficult for a number of reasons—academically, socially, emotionally. For students to grow, they must understand their weaknesses and be encouraged to advocate for themselves and their needs. Programs such as Franklin Covey's *The Leader in Me*, which was originally started by Principal Muriel Summers to improve her unsuccessful school, is a great example of how this can be done by teaching and reinforcing much-needed skills for students to understand and own who they are. Principal EL, after visiting Muriel's school and meeting with Sean Covey, introduced *The Leader in Me* at his own school with great success and still supports this program for students. Thomas Hoerr (2017), author of *The Formative Five*, addresses student advocacy directly with how students need to be taught specific skills, such as empathy, grit, and self-control. He asserts that the educational climate and structure in schools is designed for academic achievement and too often looks beyond the need for these life competencies. Like Hoerr, we contend that focusing on life skills enables students to learn more effectively and to use what they learn outside of the schooling framework. Too often, even when students acquire a skill in the classroom, they don't transfer it to other areas of life. Regardless of the program, the goal is for students to develop critical skills, such as time management, self-reflection, communication, and a host of other necessary attributes to be successful in life. These skills all center on the students ability to take ownership of who they are and what they can contribute if they value learning.

The second critical step is getting students to understanding the power of an education so that they can begin to own their learning. Schools systems must be sensitive to the fact that various programs and common processes may actually devalue the learning process or curtail students' intrinsic motivation. There is an enormous push toward college and career readiness, which we believe in deeply in terms of the intent. We champion postsecondary opportunities for students and see it as the avenue to fulfilling their dreams. However, too often it puts the cart before the horse in that the students become overly concerned with results rather than the process. Rather than appreciating their development over time, they become preoccupied with tomorrow, getting good grades, and immediate outcomes. Learning becomes about results instead of skill development and attaining concept mastery. The process of learning is overlooked and the outcome is overvalued. In addition, the very way we attempt to demonstrate learning can also negatively impact students. This is not a slam on grades and grading, but a need for a consciousness that grades should fully demonstrate competency, offer students evidence of learning in a meaningful way, and engage them in the process of iteration. There are a variety of ways to develop student ownership. Whether schools establish programs as a way to directly discuss their development through student advocacy programs, such as student-led conferences or within the classroom with reflection tools. The result has to be new opportunities for students to discuss themselves, what they are learning, how they are learning, the amount of effort they are giving, and the results they are experiencing in positive ways to ingratiate students into their own development. This takes a serious commitment and passion for getting students to see that their unique learning patterns are effective once they learn to think about the way in which they think. Metacognition over time becomes self-actualization, which is the ultimate goal before sending our students into a world where they need to find a productive place for themselves. At the highest level, they begin to do this for others as well, and it takes new opportunities for practice within and outside of the core curriculum.

The third step is for students to own their situation. To empower students and give them the tools and skills that they need to be successful, they have to have clear a understanding of their own situation in life. Students' personal situations go beyond their academic and cognitive abilities and into their home life, community surroundings, and all of the good and bad aspects of their lives. This is considered the context that students bring to school, and it's often ignored as a factor in their development. The notion is that through a deep understanding of their situation, they have the ability to persevere, exercising "grit" to go beyond the circumstances they've been dealt. Arguably most important, is that they understand what they need to move forward and that they know how to advocate for it in a productive way. Students must have the ability to bounce back from failure, recognize the challenges ahead, and use the adults in their life in a supportive manner. Positive psychology, like Martin Seligman's PERMA™ model (2018), may be a powerful tool in schools. It focuses on Positive Emotion, Engagement, Relationships, Meaning, and Accomplishments, all designed to bring about well-being and happiness. Most importantly, it touches on resilience: "It's all about one specific definition of resilience, which is optimism—appraising situations without distorting them, thinking about changes that are possible to make in your life" (Perkins-Gough, 2013). If schools work to put students in charge of their situations, we move beyond the pity that some educators have for kids and the helplessness that some families experience. An all-hands-on-deck approach requires everyone to see that the current situation doesn't have to be the future outlook.

The final step is a culminating step and it depends upon passionate school leaders who have a distinct desire for students to own their future, long after they leave us. The previous three are designed to build to the fourth, which is an understanding and belief that students need to have about their future. This step helps students to realize that learning is not arranged in a way to reach a particular destination, but rather it should act as a journey. The previous three steps are produced to build independence, helping with some of each students' immediate needs to ensure that they can soar on their own. This fourth step focuses on the future and developing skills that last for a lifetime. Essentially, "long-term interventions focus on strengthening the executive system and building a repertoire of effective self-management skills to compensate for executive weaknesses. These interventions allow our children to be competent as they move out into the world on their own" (Cooper-Kahn & Dietzel, 2009). When students learn to own their future, they quit relying on others to make it happen for them or blaming circumstances for why they haven't succeeded. They come to a realization that hard work translates to bigger rewards, and that only they have true control over what lies ahead.

Ultimately, ownership is empowerment and if students own their learning and their future, they see directly how they are responsible for it, but most importantly how they can use all the people and resources to help them achieve success, create partnerships, establish mentors, and make unique contributions as people. All of this is precipitated by adults who realize that it takes hard work to make these things happen for students and the models that we provide when we do so. It's also why we need all hands on deck with leaders to connect our work to the vision we create in our schools.

A CULTURE WHERE EVERYONE IS CONNECTED AND LEADERSHIP MATTERS

This next piece of the work ethic puzzle goes beyond the walls of the school or district office and finds itself within homes, businesses, legislative halls, community centers, churches, and any other possible support within the community. It also considers teachers as leaders and more than just instructors confined to a classroom. Belief in students must equal support, and support must come in a variety of different ways. All of the efforts around supporting and equipping students we've identified so far are necessary and maximized in what Epstein and Salinas (2004) refer to as the *school learning community,* which is "educators, students, parents, and community partners who work together to improve the school and enhance students' learning opportunities." This learning community is critical because it encompasses all stakeholders and acknowledges that student success is the responsibility of more than just the school. To embrace this, we have to fully accept the idea that schooling transcends teachers, core curriculum, time tables, and school buildings. As Sam Redding (1991) writes,

> The school is often discussed in terms of its relationship to the community suggesting that the school is something apart from the community. In fact, school exists within a mosaic of overlapping communities and is, itself capable of functioning as a community. A community is a group of people associated with one another who share common values . . . at the root, members of the school community assume responsibility for one another. (p. 9)

We have to assume responsibility for one another, and this means that we can't tolerate passengers or passive contributions to this work. Bringing together the idea that all stakeholders assume responsibility for working together as a team with leaders within the school guiding the work puts the school learning community at an advantage. In order to empower students and increase their achievement, we must take a hard look at what our students need and who they can rely on in and outside of our schools. Our reactive approach to students' needs is too slow and often too late. The biggest push in this section is to be sure that all hands are on deck; we can't afford to have people who can make a contribution sitting on the sidelines, uninvolved and admiring the hard work that others are doing.

Despite all their efforts to be responsive, schools are still predominantly designed to meet students' academic needs and rightly so. Most of the initiatives of support are added on to the existing system and lead to overburden and burnout due to the inherent limitations. As a result, the greater school community needs to truly look at what it is asking of schools and consider reframing how the school can be supported through the various agencies and centers available as local resources. Wellness centers in schools are a great example of this, but they are also overwhelmed. Schools should be equipped to provide multiple services through various agencies and people who go beyond the traditional educators in the building. In addition, schools need to creatively find ways to have community representatives in the building who may not have gone through the traditional educational route. We note two ways to get connected: create a network and influence the narrative.

CREATING A COMMUNITY OF SUPPORT BY DESIGN: NETWORKING AND STORYTELLING

1. *Creating a **network** of supports is critical.* One way to achieve this, as Epstein et. al. (2002) describe, is to coordinate resources that range from "information for students and families on community health, cultural, recreational, social support . . . to . . . one stop shopping for family services" (pp. 16, 177). The reality is that many of our schools are incredibly diverse and the demographic makeup and the cultural understanding of our students is often different than the adults who are working in the building. We attest that regardless of skin color, race, ethnicity or religion, we believe every adult has the potential to connect with any student. We

embrace that students are very open to any adult as long as they know they care. Unfortunately, there are needs that go beyond the expertise of the educators in a building. Schools should be able to rely on the outside community to help serve the children within. Until this becomes a reality and schools are fully equipped to serve as the community hub, a role in many ways they are already being asked to do, they need to fully mobilize all community support. This means reaching out to create a network, being relentless until outsiders provide, and accepting nothing less than full participation from community leaders.

2. *Write your own* **narrative story** *to influence your community and creating a strong network.* In order to build this network and build levels of support, we need to learn how to market a solid and accurate understanding of the school and what it is truly accomplishing. The outside community very often has a false understanding of what is really going on within our schools. This reality must change so that school news is not just a soundbite. We are working to change students' lives and one way to build the full story is for schools to write their own narrative. Social media is a tremendous avenue to be the source of information for your school. By leveraging various tools, schools can create an accurate picture of the school and what it is accomplishing each day. Not only can you inform the community and dispel rumors, you can also celebrate the things that are often overlooked. As a primary source of information, you create awareness, leverage, and beneficial relationships that can serve students. This approach recognizes that the school is not only a part of the community but how the community and school support one another. In *Ed Marketing: How Smart Schools Get and Keep Community Support*, the authors go beyond the idea of schools just informing the community on what's occurring to the notion that we must "establish public recognition of the issues that the school system is facing and to begin

attracting the community support for the potential recommended action" (Carroll & Carroll, 2000). This idea builds
on the notion that schools cannot function alone, and to
change the outside perception of schools, it takes a quality
marketing campaign to attract community support and
rally behind critical initiatives. Consider school climate, a
difficult topic in any school. The harsh reality is that schools
are often microcosms of the community at large and need
meaningful community connections to help solve some of
the pressing issues. However, if the community does not
have an accurate understanding of the school, any request
for outside services and help could be misconstrued. To
change the narrative regarding school climate or any other
need, the school must be transparent regarding the challenges our children face every day and leverage all possible
resources, not only to protect students at school but in the
community as well.

The key to everyone contributing is that the development of our students is the sole responsibility of simply—everyone. All components
must be in place for student success. It starts with an understanding of the power in how we treat students and learning to build the
right environment that leads to breaking cycles of failure, which calls
on educators and students to be empowered. All of this is galvanized
within a strong community that recognizes how each person can positively impact students. With that said, we still find schools that don't
creatively find ways for everyone within the school to get involved.
A mark of a quality education goes beyond the classroom, and that
means we need educators to be available for students beyond their
responsibilities within the classroom. Strong schools systems build
networks of support for students in a variety of ways. In reality, we
need to support one another and our students who need more than
just a general education if they're truly going to be successful. In the
next chapter, we outline just how that works with stories from folks
who are making it happen.

A Framework for Growth Through Reflection

Think: What Did I Learn?

Plan: What Do I Need to Do?

Act: What Will I Begin Today?

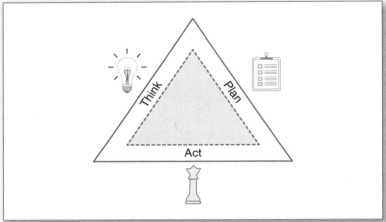

- Refer to Figure 3.1, The Difference Between a Communal Effort and an Isolated Effort, and using the descriptors, is your organization a communal culture or an isolated culture and what are some of the reasons why that may be? *Think*
- How will you shift your mindset to embrace communal efforts rather than isolated practices to be more effective in your current role? *Plan*
- What initial action steps do you need to take to design a community of support? *Action*
  - ○ Identify your *greatest challenge* regarding networking.
  - ○ Identify your *greatest opportunities* regarding networking.
  - ○ Identify your *greatest challenge* regarding telling your story.
  - ○ Identify your *greatest opportunities* regarding telling your story.

Stronger Backs,
Not Lighter Loads

"Don't be afraid to give your best to what seemingly are small jobs. Every time you conquer one it makes you that much stronger. If you do the little jobs well, the big ones will tend to take care of themselves."

—Dale Carnegie

A CONTRIBUTION IS MANDATORY

The concept is simple: everyone must make a contribution, large or small, to the overarching goal that every student shall succeed. Two things are not optional here: (1) There are no passengers on our bus. No one is passively riding along, even those doing "their job" effectively, but working in isolation. (2) All students must succeed. Why are these two concepts so important and jointly unified? Because the burden schools bear is too great without every single person committed to the goal of total success. This means that, because of quality programs and great people, every single student is ready at graduation, able to make life choices and have a variety of options because of their skill level and the fact that the school laid out all of the possibilities for them. The mission is to create a culture where everyone embraces the vision and fully accepts responsibility for student achievement, regardless of their situation and circumstance, and passionate leadership is a must for it to happen.

In the two essential areas above, we want to note that the "no passengers rule" isn't about teacher effectiveness. In our definition of work ethic and an all-hands-on-deck approach, we're assuming that the people are effective. This book is not about people who aren't performing up to standard. The three characteristics we champion as necessary for fueling passion in schools—a growth mindset, an extreme work ethic, and a positive attitude—don't consider poor performance or bad behavior. In fact, what we're saying is that the independent nature of teachers, classrooms, and schools, sometimes leaves highly effective people working in solitude, a culture that doesn't require them to contribute in new and different ways. When effective classroom teachers and leaders aren't contributing in new and innovative ways, it's usually a result of unclear goals or an insufficiently communicated vision. If we expect a culture of success, silos must fall and a true team spirit must be embraced by everyone. After all, if we expect new and different results, we have to do things differently and better, capitalizing on everyone's talents and expertise.

Passionate schools are always goal centric and learner focused. As you'll see in Chapters 5 and 6, schools need clear goals so that they can celebrate short- and long-term wins for staff and student positivity. Goals do something important as a precursor to our ability to celebrate their outcomes. They bring people together for a unified purpose and make the mission crystal clear for the people doing the work. As noted by Edmonds (2014) in *The Culture Engine*, a team's purpose and goals have to be clear, which is critical for success and even long-term survival. Although this book isn't about vision work, goal-setting, and strategic planning, having each adds the necessary clarity to fuel and sustain passion throughout an organization. It's important to realize that clear organizational goals create a stronger focus, which means there's less room for people to work in silos. Bringing people out of their silos gets them to communicate and contribute in ways that benefit all students.

For students to reach new levels of success, to eliminate any doubt regarding their own abilities, and to believe in the school community, they must have faith in the school and the adults that run it. Creating this environment helps maintain the right attitude and effort required for what Wilson and Conyers (2016) call practical optimism. "For teachers and students, developing and maintaining an optimistic outlook about learning entails staying focused on achieving positive outcomes and carrying through on action steps needed to realize those outcomes" (pp. 44–45). When this is done effectively, optimism becomes consistent and pervasive in the culture and permeates every aspect of the school. And when the adults are persistent, focusing intently on achievement, finding new avenues for students to connect and learn, the students will too. All of this is possible when the leaders demonstrate positivity, which is infectious and fun. These habits are critical if the wonders of a work ethic are going to rally the people together for success. The point is, as Achor (2013) puts it, that "you have the power to franchise positive habits in your home or workplace" (p. 194). In other words, practicing optimism, truly believing that every hurdle can be jumped over, is contagious as the flu. Our belief system as leaders, the one we described as critical from Chapter 3, can spread throughout the school and infect every adult and student if we are consistently optimistic each day. The pervasive belief and uncompromising attitude that every student must succeed draws every passionate educator to the same conclusion—we need to explore every opportunity and willingly do things uniquely different if we want to see different results in the future for our students.

To support a willingness to see and do thing differently than we've ever done them, we need to move far beyond the traditional methods of contribution that staff typically make outside of the classroom. Teachers are great with supporting administrative responsibilities. Whether stepping up to cover classes, being a hall supervisor during drills, or even serving as supports during tragic events, teachers are often available to lend a needed hand. We've worked with schools that can come together in a crisis at the drop of a hat, supporting kids and families in a particular time of need with calm and ease. The all-hands-on-deck approach we're promoting here isn't just about being available during the fire drill or even the tragic incident. We're talking about making certain that student achievement is at the center of the belief system, which means that students are connected to unique programs in and out of school, helping them succeed as learners and loving them as people. In our definition of a culture where work ethic is at the core, adults creatively search for and embrace ideas often overlooked, seemingly strange, or unfortunately uncommon but that might just work based on an individual student's academic, social, or emotional needs. What we know about high-achieving passionate schools is that they make every effort for every student to connect with the school in positive ways, and they work collectively, as a unified team, to make success a reality.

A clear indication of effective leadership is solid ownership of the goals among a cohesive team of people working toward those goals (Willink, 2017). People often say, "teamwork makes the dream work," and we alter that slightly to say, "teamwork *is the only way* that the dream will work." The power of the *I Believe* culture can only exist if teams of people are willing to go the extra mile, providing opportunities for students and taking leadership roles in schools. This leads us to the best two ways leaders create a culture where everyone contributes and makes a positive impact on students: (1) teachers using their talents beyond the classroom to offer unique and varied opportunities for students, and (2) ample opportunities for teachers to take on leadership roles throughout the school. With all hands on deck—before, during, and after school—diversifying our offerings for our diverse population of learners, every school can reach every child and achieve greatness.

MAKING A MARK: THE BEST WAYS TO MAKE AN IMPACT

To support this optimistic, value-driven environment, the school must be a high-functioning single unit that places the students well-being and achievement above all else. Developing this team mindset takes energy and optimism, but it's absolutely possible, and we've seen it in action. It takes a team effort with a passionate leader who cares deeply about the people doing the work. When Kathryn,

Lencioni's (2002) composite character, took over her team, it was dysfunctional. In some ways, it was operating counterproductively. To turn things around, she needed to develop trust, create healthy conflict around their goals and direction, improve the commitment to success, implement real accountability, and get everyone on the same page for results. She assessed the current climate, and then she got everyone moving in the same direction. For Kathryn, for the organization to be successful, everyone on the team needed to be making clear contributions to the vision, and when they weren't, she made the critical decision to dismiss them from the workload—they didn't always need to be fired, although that happens, but sometimes there's a better fit on another project.

For schools to be successful, teams need to function at their highest level, everyone must make a positive contribution, and passion is the foundation for an uncompromising work ethic. The good news about schools is that educators, by nature, possess an intrinsic desire to help, and teams are easily formed around any and all issues we uncover. Taking a team approach is about collectively coming together to solve problems, and it doesn't necessarily mean that there's one team for every decision. In fact, webs of support are much better than top-down management, even when there are clear reporting structures throughout the organization (Kotter, 2014). Teams are also important because if they are organized thoughtfully, we can maximize the strengths of a diverse group of thinkers, creating and planning for a diverse group of students. The fact is that "people from diverse backgrounds might actually alter the behavior of a group's social majority in ways that lead to improved and more accurate group thinking" (Rock & Grant, 2016). When schools employ this type of teamwork, a cross-pollination of ideas, skills, and talents, students benefit because our student population is almost always more diverse than our teaching population. This means that it's always important to use teams of leaders to make decisions, and even more important that our decisions are made with a consciousness that the student body is likely representative of a greater diversity and cultural background than our staff can provide. This approach puts unique programming, tailored to meet our students' needs, under a microscope in terms of making sure we offer what every student needs to succeed.

For our students to thrive in a diverse and ever-changing social, political, and economic world, the curriculum we teach, the extra-curricular programs we offer, and the experiences we provide them must represent their reality. This requires extreme dedication to finding new ways to meet the demands of the changing social culture from which our students come, and it requires passionate leadership at every level. Fullan (2014) reminds readers that the principal can't be the only person responsible for the intricacies of instructional leadership and curriculum design. We need teacher leaders who support the vision with every adult throughout the school in every position to step up. This can look different for everyone. It can mean taking an official role, an unofficial role, or creatively new role based on a need. The bottom line is that we need unique and captivating offerings for students, and we need staff who work together and take the lead to make that happen.

Unique Contributions to Student Learning. One thing that is making a difference in the schools that have inspired us to write this book, that are excelling at servicing the needs of an at-risk student population or otherwise just doing well with attendance, behavior, and test scores, is simply out-of-the-box programs. The words and advice from *Kids Deserve It* authors, Nesloney and Welcome (2016), are resoundingly true: "Traditions can be an important part of our schools' culture, but when it comes to learning, using decades-old tactics won't cut it. We can't expect our kids to be growing, learning, and pushing boundaries unless we're doing the same" (p. 27). Undoubtedly, there's room for much of what we've always done, and there's evidence that a great deal of it works (Ravitch, 2010), but we certainly aren't reaching all students. That's where new, unique, and different is not only important, it's our moral imperative. The good news is that we have models of reform efforts all over the country from which we can learn. We just need to build our network, learn from one another, implement brilliant ideas, and replicate programs of success in every school.

We learned from Jenna Argo, assistant principal at Phillip Showell Elementary School in Selbyville, Delaware. Her team is really thinking outside of the box to connect and engage students, and they were awarded a 21st Century Grant and partnered with University of Delaware's 4H program. The grant funding allows them to provide a unique summer and after-school program for low-income and English language learners. The students receive tutoring, complete service projects, participate in team-building activities, and even learn using LEGO robotics. Because the school recognized a need and decided to break the mold, at-risk youth are getting opportunities to learn in new ways. Traditional ways to solve problems simply won't work. For example, when students are underperforming, when test scores and proficiency rates are low, the old way to attack the problem is to consider test prep, which is only an increased focus on the problem through additional practice to improve performance. The new and unique way is to implement something altogether different than what's on the test. Phillip Showell decided to focus on enrichment and engagement. There is no doubt that learning will take place, student efficacy will grow, and strong teacher and student relationships will be formed. Notice, too, that it takes grant applications, community partnerships, and diverse thinking to make something like this work. Kudos to Phillip Showell Elementary.

Programs like the one at Phillip Showell aren't easy to get started. They take an infinite effort from a team of people. It requires optimism and faith that this new endeavor is going to work even when it hasn't been tested and requires people to make contributions in ways that they never even considered. We don't suggest, either, that all programs need to take place before or after school, although programs that extend the day serve a valuable purpose. What we're saying is that everyone, as a matter of it being mandatory, has to make a contribution outside of their regular duties as a teacher, specialist, or leader. Everyone. All hands on deck is the only path to success.

We want to introduce you to Lisa Lowe, principal of North East Elementary School in North East, Maryland. Lisa knows the power of doing things differently for the sake of student learning and the individual contributions that people must make when there's a heavy lift. North East is a Title 1 school with families who live in seriously impoverished conditions yet it also serves families with waterfront homes to the tune of millions of dollars. She told us that five years ago her team came to the realization that their state test scores were on the decline, while the number of behavior referrals was on the rise. When they disaggregated the data, low-income white males were performing the worst, but other demographic groups weren't making the grade either. They knew they had to make a change. Their story is an inspiration to all of us who willingly need to confront difficult situations and put our efforts in new directions to achieve different results for students.

Improving Student Learning in Unique Ways by Addressing Unique Needs

Lisa Lowe, Principal
North East Elementary
North East, Maryland

"When it came down to reality, it was the low-income students who were killing us . . . or maybe we were killing them. Either way, we knew something had to change, and we knew that it needed to go way beyond the canned, purchased vendor programs we were using, which had promised to fix things for us." That's how Lisa started her story when we interviewed her for the book. She said they were desperate, and nothing seemed to be working.

That's when Lisa and her team started doing research, and they began to study neurogenesis. They dove deep into brain research, and they learned that kids from poverty and trauma actually have brains that look different. "Not better or worse," she said, "just different." They learned that if they were going to be successful with their low-income population, they need to focus on five key areas: (1) vigorous physical play, (2) meaningful new learning, (3) exposure to enriched environments and experiences, (4) managed levels of stress, and (5) positive nutrition.

Lisa assembled a team of the most energetic staff members from the faculty, called the "Jedi Team." They began small and allowed the project to evolve. The first innovation was a 60-minute period of vigorous physical movement built into the students' schedule daily. "Kids who move have brains that grow" is a mantra at North East. Next, they overhauled the curriculum. At the time they started, there were kids in the fifth grade reading first-grade texts. Now, every student is exposed to at or above grade-level content. No exceptions. Lisa says that the kids simply met the challenge; one by one they improved.

Next, they literally changed the physical classroom environments. They instituted flexible seating, ball-chairs, carpeted areas, living-room-style furniture, and in the process, the students took ownership of the space. They also provided enrichment experiences with more clubs, more after school activities, and more things for students to get involved in outside of the traditional curriculum. This resulted in more students staying later into the evening than ever before. "Little do they know, while they are having fun, they are also learning," says Lisa.

To manage stress, they infused mindfulness practices into the culture. The basic philosophy is "You Matter." They began to build strong relationships by assigning particular staff members to specific students for mentoring and connectedness. They now teach yoga, de-escalation strategies, and problem-solving within the school day. The most important outcome of this work, says Lisa, is that "mindfulness taught these students that perception is reality and a positive perception often changes your outcome."

Last, and arguably most important, they tackled nutrition. Another overhaul . . . the school breakfast and lunch menu. All hands on deck means everyone, and in this case, it extended to nutritional services who were 100 percent on board. They removed any items that were high in sugar, including "the beloved chocolate milk." Lisa was also fully invested and led by example by attending a training through the Maryland Food Bank, and the school became a host site for food distribution. Each month, at North East, at no cost to the school, they have fresh healthy fruits, vegetables, and other nutritious products delivered to the school for community distribution. They grew from 2500 pounds of distributed food per month to now 8500 pounds. They also provide families with recipes to encourage healthy eating in the home with spinach and kale on the menu, foods that some families never tasted or heard of. Making it all possible, the teachers volunteer after school to facilitate the distribution and recipe discussions.

They even give away free books, host clothing swaps, dental screenings, and more. Office referrals have dropped and parental involvement has skyrocketed. The best thing for Lisa, though, is that

(Continued)

(Continued)

her staff seems happier than ever. They've realized that they're making a real difference for students, all students. Their best investment, she says, is time, energy, effort, and the attitude needed to change things in ways that they never thought were imaginable.

As a result of what they did, guess what happened at North East Elementary school? The test scores went up, which is no surprise. More important than test scores, kids started to love school, love learning, and love their teachers, knowing that the school staff is fully committed to meeting their needs as people. And, similar to all of the other stories we feature, a team of people make the difference. These passionate educators acquired new knowledge, implemented new strategies, and were consistent and pervasive with their efforts and attitudes to ensure positive outcomes. That's the wonder of a work ethic if we ever heard of one. One last thing they implemented was a pet food distribution too. We all know that kids can't learn if they're worried about their hungry cat at home. We love it. Fantastic job, North East, way to go.

5 Key Takeaways From Principal Lisa Lowe

1. *Vigorous physical play.* Principal Lowe did her research and uncovered that her students needed physical play time, and she figured out how to build that into their day. We contend that every student needs daily physical play, and the most dangerous impoverished neighborhoods prohibit that from happening after school. Take the next step in figuring out how to build time into your students' day for them to have physical activity as a core principle of learning.

2. *Meaningful new learning.* Principal Lowe went out on a limb as a single school within a system, and she instituted a curriculum

review within her school. This was outside of the norm and demonstrated bravery and courage since her students weren't making the necessary academic progress. What do you need to confront and challenge to make greater gains and have more of an impact? Instead of being a passive recipient of your district's programs and policies, add value by being at the forefront of new thinking and progressive changes. If you're thinking, "impossible, that's just going to anger the people in the district office," try anyway. Whatever the case may be, principals need to think hard about every single aspect of school and life that influences student success. Whether that be curriculum, content, instructional strategies, or community care, we need to have courage, as Lisa did, to make the difference for our kids.

3. *Exposure to enriched environments and experiences.* Transforming the classroom can be costly, but one thing that every team of teachers can do is to provide students with enriching field trip experiences. Critical to a well-rounded school curriculum is making visits to other learning environments beyond the school walls. As a passionate leader, be sure to take inventory of and support field trips for your students. If you're a school principal, challenge your teachers to provide at least one enriching field trip experience per grade for every grade level in your school. When we can't bring a new world into our classrooms, we have to consider bringing students into the world. And, the challenge of bringing the world into the classroom with new enrichment experiences can be met using technology. Students can explore beautiful and interesting places through virtual field trips like those offered through Discovery Education. When cost and logistics are reasonable, teachers should go beyond the school walls to provide unique learning experiences for their students, but when that's not feasible, we need to find ways to use technology to bring the outside world in. The key is to enrich the general curriculum with fun experiences for learning.

4. *Managed levels of stress.* Take the time to review and reflect on any strategies that your school has in place to manage student stress and well-being. Maybe you're doing Leader In Me to

(Continued)

(Continued)

demonstrate key competencies in successful thinking. Maybe you're implementing schoolwide Restorative Practices for better relationship and discipline procedures. Maybe you're including mindfulness as Principal Lowe did for her staff and students. The key takeaway is that your school may need an added layer of support for students to address mental health.

5. *Positive nutrition.* This may be the biggest fish to fry in any school. Students cannot learn effectively if they are undernourished or hungry. Restrictive federal policies, cumbersome red tape, and even a lack of healthy available food options are all major roadblocks that schools and children face. Typically school leaders see these things as outside of their purview. But that didn't stop Lisa Lowe and it shouldn't stop you. Whether you decide to take unused milk from breakfast to keep in the nurse's office for hungry students during the day or eliminate an item from the menu that you know isn't nutritious (despite it meeting guidelines), take one step in advancing your school's food choices toward better nutritional offerings for students. Do something this week.

Teacher Leadership. At the heart of every great school is a committed group of skilled, caring, and passionate staff members. It's always the staff who drive student success, school morale, and the overall working conditions. As leaders, principals have a great deal of responsibility and we firmly believe that principals should lead schools by keeping their work to vision-setting, people and program evaluation, and innovation, leaving implementation to those who actualize the work. We always say that schools should be places that are organized for teachers by teachers. Great principals know that the teachers are customers as well. If principals want teachers to provide great experiences for students, they have to provide great experiences for teachers. And decisions, as we've learned from Whitaker (2012), should be based on the best teachers and what they might think about a new idea.

We heard from Lori Quintana from Griffin Middle School in Smyrna, Georgia. She's the librarian there and clearly a leader of learning. Her story epitomizes what it means for teachers to step up when students need it most. The school set a goal for reading achievement scores to increase 5 percent annually. Through conversations among staff members, they realized this could only happen if 100 percent of the teachers were committed to reading instruction. With the support from Griffin's principal, Paul Gillihan, they did an "all call" to create a teacher-driven committee to review current reading instruction practices, and teachers stepped up from every content area. They worked through the summer to create a new framework. The entire program, designed to gets kids reading more and help teachers in all content areas teach reading strategies, is teacher created. The leadership team for this initiative, which is twenty-four strong, act as guides and mentors for the other teachers whereby 100 percent of the sixth- and seventh-grade staff are implementing the work. This is a great representation of passionate leadership where teachers and other staff members take the initiative and lead to improve student achievement. Thank you, Lori, for sharing your story and for the great work that your team is doing for kids. #GriffinReads30

We recognize the power of teacher leadership in schools, both to battle the barrage of external changes that schools manage as well as the internal initiatives, implemented to make a difference for young people. We agree with Levin and Schrum (2017) "that every teacher can learn and develop into a teacher leader" (p. 36). We assert that every teacher can step up and should have the opportunity to lead in one way or another right now. Successful teacher leadership has a great deal to do with creating small groups of teachers, at the grade level or by department, to lead various team efforts. We're calling for those common ways to lead, plus additional opportunities where each teacher, every staff member, steps up to lead and contribute in a positive way. This can vary from being a committee chairperson, leading a new initiative, being the iPad go-to person, or being the official testing coordinator. The point is that schools have an incredible need for help with limitless opportunities where everyone must contribute to achieve the school's vision.

Taylor Armstrong told us a great story about teacher leaders that had the trickle-down effect that passionate school systems create when leadership is systematic. Taylor was the technology coordinator for Talladega City Schools in Alabama when this all unfolded. Taylor supported eight schools with their tech implementation, which meant he needed help to manage the devices, train teachers, disseminate any new programs, and translate ideas into action. Teacher leaders were the perfect solution for this, but wait to you hear who took the lead along the way.

Using a Team Approach to 1:1 Integration

Taylor Armstrong, Technology Coordinator
Talladega City Schools
Talladega, Alabama

When Taylor Armstrong realized that the STEM initiative and the 1:1 rollout were happening simultaneously, he knew he needed help. He was flying solo, supporting eight schools, including a career and technical school as well as an alternative school, with all of their technology needs. There was no way that he could be expected to operate without some assistance, but there wasn't money in the budget to hire new technology specialists, and Taylor didn't need just a few; he needed an army.

That's when he reached out to the principals of the schools and asked for help. His first idea was to get someone at each school to lead the initiative, and he pulled together enough money to pay each of them a stipend. He asked the principals for a name or two of someone who they thought would be a good fit as a leader in the school. He needed buy-in, trust, and influence. He needed leadership.

The principals quickly provided names of teachers who they believed could be an asset in leading the initiative. Taylor ran with the names, contacted each of them, and no one turned him down. And it wasn't about the meager stipend; that was just somewhat of a "thank you" for taking the role. Rather, "they were dying to help make their schools better," Taylor said. They named the position *tech assistants*.

Next, he brought the team together for trainings. He paid for substitute teachers and unified the group to learn together, ask questions, and support one another. They met about every nine weeks, and during the time in between, they used Voxer to communicate and support one another. The teacher leaders became their own network so that they could ensure a smooth 1:1 roll out and support their respective schools. It was working beautifully.

The best part is that the teachers trained student-leaders at all of the schools to help as well. The leadership aspect effectively trickled down from Taylor to the teacher leaders to the student leaders, called *techsperts*. The techsperts were honored with certificates at board meetings throughout the year to demonstrate appreciation for their leadership. In the end, Taylor found the students often knew more than the teachers, which allowed the teachers to do more facilitation than anything else. A perfect picture of leadership in schools and passion at its core.

Taylor's story demonstrates passionate leadership, and it exemplifies creatively finding solutions, supporting an initiative through leadership, and truly modeling all hands on deck. Taylor modeled for the teachers, the teachers modeled for the students, and everyone contributed to the success of the initiatives by willingly leading their critical part of the program. When people step up into a leadership role and have a clear purpose, it creates excitement and energy, which fuels the passion and desire to add value. In turn, this passion spreads through to everyone else. In fact, teacher leadership may actually be the silver bullet everyone is looking for to fix all of our problems in schools. Great leaders know that the best management strategy, hands down, is to find the right people, with the right strengths to take the lead, and then get the heck out of their way.

4 Key Takeaways From Taylor Armstrong

1. *You can't lead alone.* Hopefully this stands out as a theme from this book that leadership is a team effort, and schools need all hands on deck. Taylor knew that he couldn't handle the implementation

(Continued)

(Continued)

on his own so he reached out for help. The first step in sustaining excellence is realizing that you can't move huge boulders without a team of people. Reflect on your major projects to determine if you're trying to do too much without the necessary help needed for your work to be successful.

2. *Identify key people.* Once you've realized that you need a team, identifying key people is a must. Notice that Taylor didn't select the people himself. He reached out to the school principals for input. Obviously Taylor couldn't have known all of the key people to do the selecting himself, but that's not the major reason to allow others to make the selection. By reaching out to others to help identify key people, we build trust, communicate that we're all part of the process, and create ownership. Giving the principals the selection authority created the culture needed for everyone to be involved. The alternative is that when something goes wrong, you're likely to hear, "Well that's not my problem, and I wouldn't have even picked that person anyway." The key takeaway is that whenever you are looking to identify key people, get input and go with it.

3. *Invest in your leaders.* Once Taylor had the key people selected, he built a system that developed them as leaders. He didn't do a single one-off PD offering. Instead, he connected the leaders through the use of technology so that their questions and issues could be tackled through support and communication. Not only does investing in your people support their efforts and grow them to get better, it acts as a retention strategy to keep them aware of changes, clear on expectations, and motivated to continue the mission. If there's a key takeaway that we all need to keep as a focus, it's invest in your people.

4. *Celebrate success.* One of our favorite aspects of the Taylor Armstrong story is how he consistently and systematically celebrated the people. Celebrations is the entire focus of the last section of this book (Part III), and Taylor's work highlights how important it is. When we originally heard from Taylor, we assumed that he celebrated this effort at one board meeting. He clarified that they celebrated every month with certificates and applause for the teacher and student work. The key takeaway is that we need more frequent and systematic celebrations.

SYSTEMATIZING STRENGTHS

A culture of passion is one where we systematize to maximize our strengths and manage ourselves to minimize our weaknesses. That's not to say that we ignore our deficits, but it does mean that we focus on our strengths as the best path to success. Clifton and Nelson (1992) describe the power of focusing on strengths, which is best captured by an interview conducted with the incredible 1984 Chinese ping pong Olympic gold winners who said, "if you develop your strengths to the maximum, the strengths become so great it overwhelms the weaknesses" (p. 19). Interestingly some of the team members had noticeable weaknesses that opponents simply could not overcome. This same philosophy applies to students and staff who can reach unprecedented achievements, but who, at times, need reminders about knowing and maximizing their strengths. This is forged in a growth mindset to manage situations effectively and optimistically.

Making a unique contribution to student learning can only be systematized when we know the strengths of the staff and put those strengths to work, in pursuit of doing something new and different for maximum results. We operate from the belief that everyone has something unique to contribute, and passionate leaders tap into the unique attributes of everyone on the team. This might sound simple, but it's easier said than done. That's because of our mindset. Most of us, even our best team players, "undervalue what we inherently do well" (Johnson, 2018). For this reason, leaders have to explicitly create opportunities for involvement and recognize the contributions that people make.

The same goes for students. Students need to know that they have a welcoming and supportive place to grow and learn where hard work is expected, rewarded, and honored. We need to be clear that every child must be challenged, regardless of that child's ability level. This means that we need to find more challenging work for the ones who breeze through and praise everyone else for sticking with it (Duckworth, 2016). This requires us to totally rethink how we view our students' performance and the language we use to support their effort and growth. We're generally accustom to praising them for a job well done, but only recognizing the completed project does not place the appropriate value on their hard work and effort throughout the learning process.

> Students need reminders that a poor score on one test does not mean they will never master the lesson content. They need to hear that setbacks offer learning opportunities and that they can improve their performance by steadily developing their knowledge and abilities. (Wilson & Conyers, 2016, p. 38)

One of the greatest leadership lessons one might find is what we can learn from failure, yet our culture still doesn't value it like we should. Pushing past an obstacle is a wonderful attribute, and anyone "who is unable to get over previous hurts and failures is held hostage by the past" (Maxwell, 2000, p. 77). It takes passionate leaders to inspire growth, hard work, and positivity in people, especially when we're faced with roadblocks and pitfalls. This is why we need schools filled with staff who are willing to make a unique contribution and build our army of teacher leaders to improve student learning in our schools.

DEFINING THE ROLES AND NAMING THE POSITIONS

Erickson (2008) challenges the need for titles in the workplace. She does so using the basic premise that *half* of the reason we use titles is to recognize upward mobility and the progress that folks have made in their careers. She claims, though, that this can also have a negative impact, essentially locking people into "levels of compensation and assumed prestige." A number of other works make similar assertions, where titles equate to hierarchy, and hierarchy is associated with pay, authority, and control. But, in education, the corporate ladder doesn't exist, and there are only a handful of jobs outside of the classroom.

In fact, in education, when everyone ends up with the same title, "teacher," "counselor," "specialist," why would we even concern ourselves with the concept? On the contrary, there's good reason to do so in schools. We advocate for giving people secondary titles that differentiate and identify the functions of support that people provide based on their strengths beyond their predominant role. Because so many people carry the same title, defining and naming their other roles is the only way we can know who the go-to people are for help. This, Erickson argues, is the other *half* of having a title, which she supports, because it tells everyone "to whom they should look for specific actions and decisions."

We see titles as critically important to associating people with the work being done and defining the roles that people play outside of the classroom. When staff members make a unique contribution by doing something, based on individual strengths, we find it to be important to give them credit for their efforts and make it known to others. Recognition only works when it's systematized, when it's specific to a person, and when it's limited to a unique contribution (Gostick & Elton, 2009). We're taking recognition to the next level by saying that the additional role should be written right into the titles of the people in the school. Everyone needs a secondary title that demonstrates their contribution or their leadership position. This also notes, explicitly, for the staff that we're looking for everyone to commit to adding value outside of their primary title. We break these titles into three separate categories.

Official Titles. These are paid positions like a department chairperson or a grade-level leader. Tech assistants, used by Taylor Armstrong in our last story, is a perfect example of an official title. The teachers in those positions were paid, and they had a title to differentiate their contribution, letting everyone know who to go to for tech support. Any number of functions in a school can have an official title with a small agreed-upon stipend for the work. It shows appreciation and value.

Unofficial Titles. These are nonpaid volunteer positions, but nonetheless critically important to the school's mission. Everyone should have an unofficial title, which could be as simple as the yearly 5K coordinator (the person who takes the lead on the yearly 5K fundraiser) or eighth-grade PLC leader (the person who writes the agenda for the PLC and who takes the notes) or even parent pickup officer (the person who consistently helps with buses and after school pickup, even in the rain). These titles are important, and they demonstrate that we are all adding distinct value. In Lisa Lowe's example, her team was dubbed the Jedi Team; who doesn't want to have a title for peace and justice?

Creative and Fun Titles. These are a flavor of the unofficial titles whereby people get to provide their own self-proclaimed title or they might inherit a title from their team. They are not to be confused with silly nicknames, but rather indicate the value and contribution that one makes. Giving the kids "techspert" titles is a perfect example. If you think this may be frivolous or worse yet, unnecessary, consider the research. In *Alive at Work: The Neuroscience of Helping Your People Love What They Do,* Cable (2018) demonstrates the powerful effect of retitling employees with creative and self-reflective descriptions on the job, which effectively increases worker satisfaction, productivity, creativity, and coping with stress. These fun titles might be more important than our official ones.

We're so serious about this that we want you to put these titles on name plates and e-mail signatures. We also believe that every

Figure 4.1   Unique Contributions Model

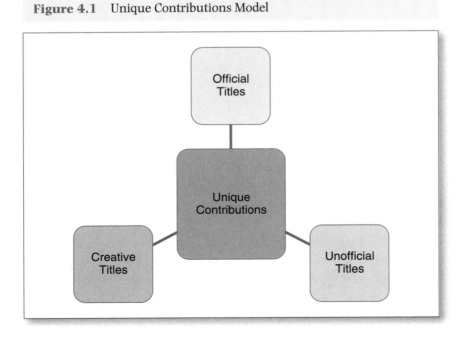

educator should have a business card, from the main office secretary to the chief custodian, everyone contributes because everyone has an impact.

EVERYBODY MAKES A DIFFERENCE

As principal, T.J. and his team implemented a number of unique programs. One of which included a culinary, middle school talent-development period. The program was new and unique because, at the time, middle schools in the district didn't offer culinary arts, but the team was willing to come together for students who wanted to try their skills at cooking. The heroes who led the program were the kitchen manager and the school nurse who taught the period together, which was every Thursday. Students met in the school kitchen for lessons, demonstrations, and practical experience. The kitchen manager taught culinary skills, like how to grip a knife, equipment setup, and ingredient portioning. The nurse taught the concepts of dietary needs and nutrition. The program culminated in a cook-off with guest judges from local restaurants. Kids presented a meal from a recipe that they planned, portioned, and executed in the kitchen. Of course, everyone was a winner. The real accomplishment, though, was that the school found an opportunity to offer something that engaged students in a new way, taught them new skills, and showed them how to contribute at home in the kitchen, which will benefit them with the lifelong knowledge and habits that are required for meal planning and healthy living.

That's what we mean by everyone contributes. The kitchen manager became a culinary instructor and the school nurse became a child nutritionist. In this example, people took on nontraditional roles, outside of their typical contribution, to make a difference for students that will last a lifetime. The idea is that everyone has strengths, hobbies, personal projects, and expertise that lend to unique opportunities for kids—before, during, and after school. In Chapter 6, we note the power of after-school programs, and here we preface that with the fact that everyone has to get involved in ways that make schools a skill depot and not just a general curriculum factory.

TECHNICAL TIP #1: SURVEY FOR STRENGTHS, HOBBIES, AND FUN PROJECTS

Every initiative needs energy, and to get new things going, we suggest surveying the staff at the beginning and end of every year. At the beginning of the year, ideas are fresh and the staff is energized and excited, while at the end of the year, the staff can reflect and add insight and value that allows the administrative team to review over the summer and prepare for the upcoming year. The survey should be quick and easy, requiring only about ten minutes to complete, with three sections for open-ended responses. The three areas will provide insight into ways in which the staff may contribute that you didn't even know about and it provides them an opportunity to share their strengths and ideas.

1. *What activities, hobbies, or projects are you interested in that might also interest our students?* This question is used to get them thinking about their personal interests that might be a good fit for the school. One year when T.J. surveyed his staff, a few staff members wrote "running," which prompted a running club. None of the teachers who wrote that they enjoyed running wanted to lead a running club alone, but collectively they were able to breathe life into it. So twice a week, students and staff met at the flagpole after school and they went running together. It created a sense of belonging, it was a healthy outlet, and it was a unique contribution to the culture that they might not have otherwise made without the survey.

How-To: Use a *Google Form* to survey the staff and collect and catalog the data. Staff can submit the form as a matter of their checkout items for the summer. As a leader, this is also a way to get to know the staff a bit better. Use the summer months to review the information, make connections, and begin the school year with your additional programs and activities.

2. *What unofficial or new leadership role might you be able to take on at school?* This question is used to get staff members to think about a role that they can fulfill outside of their title. First, it explicitly emphasizes the administration's goal that everyone

leads in some capacity, and second, it provides insight to how people view themselves as leaders and potential roles they may fill. You might find that someone is willing to serve on a committee that they just didn't feel "invited" to in the past.

How-To: Above the open-ended item in your *Google Form*, list all of the current unofficial leadership titles held in your school along with every committee that meets throughout the year. Allowing staff to review the list will prompt them to visualize themselves in one of the positions or serving on one of the committees. Provide them with something to think about as they respond.

---

3. *What official leadership role do you believe would suit you in the future?* This question truly is about the future and succession planning. We have official titled leadership roles in schools, and we often don't think about filling them until the grade-level leader or department chair steps down. This type of survey question gathers important information about who might view themselves as potential leaders, which not only allows you to plan for future positions, it allows you to design and tailor your leadership development for certain individuals.

How-To: Make a note on the *Google Form* that this is not about replacing current staff but rather for planning for the future. Be explicit. First, we don't want to scare or create doubt among our current leaders. And, second, we don't want to put folks in the position to think that they're going to take something away from another person. If you note, right in the question stem, that this is about succession planning and leadership development, you'll get a candid response.

Providing the staff the opportunity to self-reflect and share ideas gives them an opportunity to reveal what they can contribute through hard work and discretionary effort. Here, you're not asking people to do something extra, you're asking them what they think they might be able to do that will contribute to the success of the students and the school. Those are two totally different tactics, and in a culture of contribution, it's far better to get volunteers than to coerce people into doing something new and different. These types of surveys collect really powerful data about the people in our organizations and their personal interests and professional leadership aptitude, information you need to know to be a passionate leader.

TECHNICAL TIP #2: HIRING CONTRIBUTORS

The evidence is clear that if we're going to reach all students and truly make a difference, we have to do things differently. That means we need people on the team who can make unique contributions and we need leaders to step up and show the way. Everyone must exhibit the wonders of a work ethic. Although we can motivate people to work harder, contribute more, think differently, and display passion, it's actually easier to make these things a prerequisite for employment in schools. Here are three practical strategies to improve hiring practices so that you can cast a net for people who have a strong work ethic.

1. *Add it to the job description.* Something should be in your job descriptions that tells applicants that you're looking for passion and hard work. *We're looking for people who want to make a difference and who know that it takes an extreme effort to do so. We need unique contributors and innovative thinkers. We want your ideas, we want to do things differently, and we need a team of leaders to get us where we are going. If you enjoy the status quo, please do not apply.* We like job descriptions that are precise, telling applicants what you're looking for, why it's important to you, and even who is not a good fit.

2. *Ask for examples in the interview.* Ask candidates to explain a unique program that they started, a leadership position that they held, and something they plan to do as a unique contribution if they get the job. Listen for projects and programs that are extraordinary, maybe something that no one on the interview panel has even heard before. Listen also for ways in which the person contributes outside of his title and personal endeavors that take time and energy to accomplish. You'll see the differences between candidates unfold in front of you.

3. *Use a scenario as a test.* Provide an example of a problem-of-practice and see if candidates can think beyond the general solutions of the past. See if someone on your list surprises you with an idea that is way outside of the box.

Hiring the right staff members to join your team is not easy, and screening for work ethic is tough, but it's a critical area of passion that you need to know about before you offer someone a job in your school. People who are willing to think differently and step up into leadership roles are the ones who will take your culture to the next level, and they'll be the ones who create opportunities for students worth celebrating.

A Framework for Growth Through Reflection

Think: What Did I Learn?

Plan: What Do I Need to Do?

Act: What Will I Begin Today?

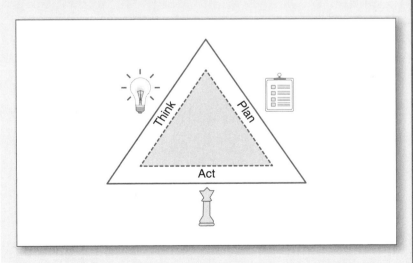

(Continued)

(Continued)

- What is one thing that you can do to improve student learning by addressing the unique needs of your learners? *Think*
- As you plan to conduct a survey of the staff, what are three questions that you can ask that will generate information about their strengths, areas of interest, and leadership potential? *Plan*
- What is the first step that you will take to create a culture where everyone makes a unique contribution? *Action*

Part III
Positivity Fueled by Celebrations
Beyond the Basics

"Education is the most powerful weapon you can use to change the world."

—Nelson Mandela

Our strength is our belief that each child can learn and succeed despite circumstance. There is a desperate need for the thread that we use to weave the fabric of our schools to be made from the essence of care and compassion. Unconditional faith and belief, regardless of situation and circumstance, is the foundation for success in life, business, and the ideal on which we educate students. It's only in an environment where principals believe in and support teachers, and teachers who trust and support principals, can we empower students to be and do their best. They live by the mantra that *Today I will lift people through positivity*. Each year, over fifty million students fill our schools, and our classrooms, and they enter our halls needing us to be motivated and passionate people as their teachers and leaders, and this has to be despite the variety of circumstances, situations, adversities, and challenges they bring. It's the stories we tell, like the one about Susan and Chris, that make educators want to celebrate everything about what it means to be an educator.

Inspiring Hope Through Passionate Educators
Success Is Possible Regardless of Circumstance

Susan and Chris, Students
Wilmington, Delaware

Susan and Chris, brother and sister, twins no less, were in serious need for their school to be more than a place to learn; they needed stability, high expectations, opportunities, and staff who cared about their success in life. More than anything, they needed a place to call home.

For Susan and Chris, any semblance of a dinner-table conversation occurred during A-lunch at 11 a.m.—a time to catch up and see how the other one was doing. Eating together at night, under the same roof, was no longer possible. Since they took different classes in the vocational technical school they attended and were in different career programs, even lunch together wasn't always easy, and that's when a quick hug in the hallway was a must.

It sounds odd, but for Susan and Chris, the only chance they had to really see each other was during the school day. In the eighth grade, their world fell apart with a shattered home, parents not around, and at once they found themselves on the street, homeless. All the details to how and why are blurry, even to Susan and Chris, but through the kindness of others, they always found places to stay, only rarely together, as siblings should be.

With all of the chaos around them, for Susan and Chris, school was a safe haven—a place not only to learn, but one of comfort, stability, and normalcy. For their four years of high school, they attended regularly, did their work, and prepared to walk across the stage at graduation. They were always together during the day at some point, but each experienced differing challenges in the evenings and into the night. As their names were called, they received their diplomas, and accepted this great accomplishment with hope in their hearts. A hope that wasn't always there. It was only the very few teachers and school officials who knew their story and what they overcame to reach this milestone in life. For those who really knew Susan and Chris, the passion welled and great cheer came from the audience as they made their way across the stage, one after the other.

Nearly four thousand people filled the arena to watch and celebrate the graduating class. For ninety minutes, all the attention, celebration, and recognition was on the students. In this moment, nothing is more important than receiving a diploma and being recognized for all of the hard work it takes to earn the degree. As three hundred and eighty-seven students walked across the stage that night, all fulfilling a thirteen-year journey of learning, Susan and Chris knew that it was more than special for them. Each student carries with them their own unique story, but for these two, it was all about the fact that school had become their home, the only place where they could be together as sister and brother. It was where every adult who touched their lives became a parent, supporting their needs as they learned more than their subjects and report cards could examine.

They celebrated their successes with one another and all the challenges faded away. As the names were read, Susan and Chris among them, it pulled on the heartstrings of the educators in the audience who had the passion to make sure that every student in that auditorium felt special, and cared for, just enough to make it there. The people in the audience who had made it happen for Susan and Chris, given all of their trials and tribulations along the way, needed only that night, to watch them cross the stage, to fuel their passion to continue to do what schools do best for kids.

Susan and Chris found a home in their school that offered care, support, and real opportunities for success. In schools, we don't always know the circumstances behind the happy smile, the angry face, or any other emotion that kids bring with them each day. As leaders, what we know is that each of our students needs someone to care for them, someone willing to go above and beyond to ensure that they have the opportunity to learn and find their way to graduation successfully. Schools aren't just a place with books, computers, assignments, and homework. When passion thrives in schools, they can become a place where everyone feels at home, treating the cafeteria as a real dining room, and inspiring a kind of positivity that people need to be their best. It takes commitment, and it's the truly positive educators who can ignite a system.

Committing to a Culture of Celebration

"Our chief want is someone who will inspire us to be what we know we could be."

—Ralph Waldo Emerson

THE POWER OF CONNECTION

Have you ever felt the raw power of synergy? Work feels effortless, ideas come easy, collaboration is inspiring, and work becomes fun. That's the result of a clear purpose. Purpose creates connections between people, which creates synergy whereby outcomes are the collective effort of a group versus the individual contributions of the group members. The positivity that ensues is endless, and it's celebrations that fuel the positivity that comes from purpose and synergy. In some of the most important works on positive culture, we find goal setting and communication at the core. In fact, two significant drivers for people are having clear goals (Blanchard & Bowles, 1998) and communicating a clear why (Sinek, 2011), but challenges still remain when attempting to motivate people, to keep them on track, and to sustain a rapid pace. Staff need energy, encouragement, and a positive outlook. This necessary fuel, created by the work, can be found in the power of recognizing those who contribute daily to living out the mission and vision of the organization. In fact, celebrations are a common occurrence in our society. Whether birthdays, the New Year, retirements, or special accomplishments, people enjoy the social aspect of recognizing others, singling out a day or moment that makes people feel special. But celebrations are not just important as social events; they're also a critical aspect of any professional culture. Well-developed systems of recognition and celebrations have the potential to connect people to one another and their work. This connection, as Dr. Hallowell (2011) states, is crucial because when a "person connects with another person or a task, his mind changes for the better" (p. 86). The mind changes for the positive. The best schools are committed to a positive mindset by creating a culture where connections are vital, celebrations are a norm, and passion is fuel for the people.

Some associate celebrations in schools with play or time off task, believing there is too little time to spend it celebrating or that celebrations detract from the "real" work at hand. The worst of such beliefs is that there really is not much to celebrate anyway so why bother. This mindset is destructive to the overall organization and any semblance of positive culture. It reveals a fundamental misunderstanding that schools represent far more than content and test scores. Schools are living breathing ecosystems where true purpose cannot be created through policy and where meaning is not generated through mandates. Passionate schools are built on the old adage that people don't care how much you know until they know how much you care. Great schools thrive through relationships, and great school systems are a network of connections, intertwined together, to ultimately support teachers and benefit students. When teachers lack support, schools suffer, and when school systems suffer, the people in them lose their passion. Without passion, people quickly become disengaged with the work. In fact, a 2012 Gallup poll of 7,200 teachers revealed the staggering result that "nearly 70% [of teachers] are not engaged in their jobs" (Gallup, 2014, p. 26).

This lack of engagement, essentially a lack of meaningful connection to their work, is devastating to the schools they teach in, to the students they instruct, and also to themselves. The problem is that teachers don't start out this way. We have yet to meet a teacher that enters the profession demonstrating a deficit in passion and the desire to connect with their students and school community. The opposite is true: Teachers enter the profession to make a difference, not only for each individual child they teach, but for the community as a whole. The disengagement is the result of a variety of factors both internally and externally, but it creates passionless experiences and doesn't promote positivity in schools. Whether feeling unsupported, working in isolation, being underappreciated, or not having a voice, the result is disconnection, disengagement, and discontent. The outcome of teaching, working in schools, should be an attitude of gratitude, a position of positivity, and not the other way around. We have to do something about it or things won't change.

THE REVOLVING DOOR

Consider one dire result of this disengagement that is crushing many schools—teachers leaving the profession, early and in droves. Teacher turnover fluctuates greatly from state to state and from situation to situation, but teacher turnover is highest in those schools and situations where greater support is needed. Title I schools, special education settings, and high-need areas, such as world language and STEM-related jobs, experience incredibly high rates of turnover (Carver-Thomas & Darling-Hammond, 2017). The question is why are teachers leaving when the profession can be so rewarding? There are always a variety of factors to why people leave their jobs, such as relocation and retirement, but the stark reality in education is that it can be boiled down to dissatisfaction. Lack of support, federal and state accountability pressures, and poor working conditions top the list. High teacher turnover and the inability of districts to attract teachers fresh from preservice programs is an ongoing issue. The revolving door in schools crushes support for educator development and student achievement, dubbing this a true crisis.

For success to be achieved, teacher retention must improve, and the first step is ensuring that there is a connection made between the teacher and the school where she works. In the thought provoking leadership book, *Spark,* Angie Morgan and colleagues detail a time at The Basic School, where newly appointed and commissioned United States Marine Corp officers are taught how to be Officers of Marines. She explains that during her time in the rigorous six-month training school, she experienced a death in the family and this is when she truly understood that compassion and understanding are not incompatible with high standards and extreme accountability. She learned from her superior officer that as a leader "you can be tough, you can be aggressive, you can have demanding standards—but if you can't be compassionate, empathetic, and caring, you're never going to build a team of people that feel valued and connected" (p. 127). For certain, we can't imagine an environment where this is more necessary than in the Marines, where service can potentially mean sacrificing your life. But, school systems can adopt the same mentality of pressure and support by creating an effective culture grounded in the belief that teachers and schools are making a difference, that they can achieve great results, overcome odds, and meet the needs of every child. It's not going to happen without compassion for people or a positive outlook on the demands and challenges of the work. And, it's definitely not going to happen by creating a pressure cooker that doesn't have a release valve. We can't continue to push down without also lifting up.

YOU CAN'T LIFT ANYTHING UP
WHILE YOU'RE PUSHING IT DOWN

If you want to lift anything from the point where it touches a surface, you need to generate enough force to offset gravity, which offers a constant resistance of 9.8 m/s squared downward. Objects that have no momentum require greater force to move than objects already in motion, and as Newton's laws have taught us, it's easier to stay in motion than to move from a point of stagnation. When objects are too big or too heavy, we can employ the use of levers to help get them into forward motion. Ideas that are morphed into initiatives to reach goals are no different. In fact, we can learn a lot from the natural laws of science in order to lead more effectively. This is where scientific principles meet social endeavors. We must use energy and force to lift our school culture, which always comes in the form of support, positivity, and celebration. This is what creates and sustains positive momentum forward for a school.

Unfortunately, education experiences the opposite. In fact, we can liken it more to the quote often attributed to Captain Bligh of the *Bounty*, "the beatings will continue until morale improves." Education always is a political and economic focal point at the local, state, and federal levels. This can be a powerful force for the positive, but too often the message is negative—our nation's schools are underperforming and under preparing our students for the future with serious global implications. This sentiment is not new— whether we look at the article in the 1958 *Life* magazine titled, *Crisis in Education*, or the recent 2008 documentary (Compton, 2008) titled, *2 Million Minutes*—over the last fifty-plus years, various messages portray education in a negative light and hold that our systems don't live up to international standards and as a result will not compete on a global level. A *Crisis in Education* depicted two students, one from Moscow and one from Chicago, and how the American student was less focused on academics and his future, compared to his Russian counterpart. Fifty years later, the film *2 Million Minutes* compares U.S. high school students with their international counterparts from India and China.

Undoubtedly, we can learn from great systems and great organizations nationally and internationally. Identifying "bright spots" in other systems and cherry-picking them to improve a school and student achievement is what many successful schools do. However, the traditional American approach to school reform highlights the negative and focuses on weaknesses to improve performance. This call-to-action approach for school improvement is ineffective and potentially alienates those in the profession. School reform cannot be initiated from a place of intimidation and power. Fear and consequence may yield short-term results by generating activity, but this tactic often lacks the depth of true transformative advancement. Long-term results are fueled and sustained by bridging people and their work, creating commitment, and developing resilience to achieve new heights amid all the challenges, distractions, and hardships faced every day in our schools.

It is absolutely necessary for schools to be centered on student achievement and there is a place for federal and state accountability. Having high standards and clear goals to measure our progress and success at various levels is essential to gain a pulse on student competencies with core subject matter. At the same rate, we must acknowledge that general standards of proficiency and high-stakes testing lose an element of sensitivity to diversity within every school. As Behar and Goldstein (2009) write in *It's Not About the Coffee*, early in the days of Starbucks as a start-up, the executives were totally focused on being "coffee experts," and, in turn, their customer service was awful. One letter to the CEO depicted the company as not caring about people, declaring "apparently customers are not important to you." At the beginning of their identity development, Starbucks got wrapped up in their coffee and lost sight of their customers. As Behar and Goldstein state, "we got swept up in our passion for the product instead of our passion for the people" (p. 71). This is similar to our approach to student achievement. We forget about the human side to our profession and invest more in the outcomes and not enough in the culture needed to produce those outcomes.

If students are not meeting basic standards of proficiency in core subject areas, schools have to dig deep into the data and their current practices to make the right changes for the sake of kids. In fact, the science of educating young people is becoming clearer, and brain research is telling us more and more about the practices we can use for teaching and learning, and ultimately for retention and skill development. Schools who fail to recognize and implement the tactics and tools that work best, grasping to improve the past without innovation and change, will continue to fall under measures of accountability. Schools of the future, who choose to thrive, will be the ones who embrace research- and evidence-based practices that work. But, practices are not the only thing that equates to quality schooling or even a high degree of achievement. It's schools that recognize proficiency scores and annual assessment as only one measure for celebration and find multiple definitions of "success" that will embody the culture necessary to inspire passion.

So the same laws that apply to the natural world can be applied to that of improving schools. The greatest levers for lifting school culture are recognizing the great work being done in the schools, encouraging teachers and support staff, and finding ways to duplicate stories of success for everyone. We cannot define our schools with simple measures, and we have to sustain a positive environment for passion and a greater purpose.

THERE'S MORE THAN ONE WAY TO DEFINE SUCCESS

We can learn a valuable lesson from professional sports, which are known for their culminating championship events to determine success and declare victors. However, this one marquee event that crowns a champion does not discredit the entire season for others. Many accomplishments and victories are heralded throughout. Although Wimbledon is often considered the marquee grand slam tournament, it doesn't disqualify the other tournaments or their respective champions. The World Cup is played every four years with the desire to improve the international sport of football and serve the fans. But, the sport itself is greater than the individual teams, and although the focus is on the winner, the glory is in the pursuit of the games. Loss doesn't always mean failure if great strides were made and the teams, players, and challengers won the hearts of the fans and made gains on the field.

The National Football League has several distinct accolades to honor and celebrate achievements throughout a season. There is no doubt that every team wants to win the Super Bowl, but of the thirty-two teams that take the field each year, there can only be one champion. Something fascinating, though, is the Coach of the Year selection. You would think that the Coach of the Year would be the coach who won the big game, taking his team all the way. Yet, that's not the case. In fact, the Coach of the Year award is based on the success and accomplishments of the team made throughout the season. Since the official merger of the NFL in 1970, only seven of the coaches who won the coveted Coach of the Year award were also Super Bowl winners. Although the ultimate goal is to win the Super Bowl, the difference in the coaching award lies in the established criteria, which considers the unique nature and talents of each team. The award recognizes the outstanding accomplishments, strides made, and small wins throughout the entire season. It demonstrates success in a number of areas over time rather than just "winning."

Our criteria and reason for "celebrating" and evaluating our schools is too often measured solely on the big game—high-stake assessment results grounded in federal and state accountability. This approach ignores the tremendous accomplishments made by many schools throughout any given school year but who still may fall short of the preidentified accountability measures that are often outwardly imposed. Sadly, many schools that have made great strides are still viewed as failing and considered ineffective. The real outcome of this method of school evaluation is that the trust between the school and outside agencies is severed because this type of accountability does not appear to be aligned with the reality of the progress being made. The internal and external definitions of success are often conflicting, and since incremental gains may not yield the ultimate prize, nothing is celebrated. Unlike the positive nature that separates the NFL's Coach of the Year award from the Super Bowl, schools don't often have such measures to reward anything other than the end game.

LEADERSHIP: CHOOSING YOUR DIRECTION

Despite this reality, schools driven by passion understand the science behind celebrating great work, and they build environments that recognize a variety of different accomplishments to forge strong relationships among the staff and their work. This does not suggest that there is not an honest gut-check reality of what needs to be achieved, or the work that needs to be done, for kids to be proficient. Rather, it recognizes the intricacies involved each step of the way and that the road of success is difficult, so support (celebration) is critical for a culture of positivity. Are there obstacles to overcome? Yes. Are there schools that need serious help and intervention? Yes. Is there room to improve? Yes. Every school must go through the process of identifying their goals, evaluating their achievement, and ensuring the alignment between their efforts and the actions necessary to meet their goals (Blanchard & Johnson, 1982). However, just like the incredible boat captain who can sail onward, regardless of the wind direction, through careful maneuvering and a great crew, so can schools create passion about students and their success, despite the direction of the outside pressures. Great school leaders build relationships, and they know how to right the sails in order to capture the wind needed to support teachers, celebrate success, and build a positive environment, regardless of the conditions.

CHARTING THE DIFFERENCE

Consider the vastly different approach detailed in the chart below. What teachers experience in schools can be driven by passion and celebration versus what research about school environments is demonstrating—little support, overwhelming accountability measures, and a lack of celebration. For school leaders, it's almost never about *what* we do but *how* we do it. Leading through positivity and celebration means tweaking practices to include a greater connection among people.

Take, for example, two of the descriptions in the chart: *interdependent* and *supported* versus *isolated* and *stunted*. A school that values *interdependence* builds systems for teachers to observe and learn from one another. A school that doesn't value frequent visits to classrooms by teachers and leaders allows educators to remain *isolated* for most of the school year. A school where teachers are *supported* provides ample opportunity for professional growth through both feedback and development. Whereas, a school that *stunts* teachers does the opposite, providing little time to improve practices, thwarting and even reversing any positive momentum in performance.

We offer this chart to demonstrate that the shift is not so daunting. It takes strong leadership and a vision for a passionate school where positive people thrive. It certainly takes strong cycles toward measures of improvement and hard work, and it's marked by short-term wins and dashboards that demonstrate success in the interim.

Figure 5.1 The Difference Between a Culture of Celebration and Culture of Neglect

Celebrated	*versus*	Ignored and Admonished
Autonomous		Abandoned
Interdependent		Isolated
Praised		Punished
Collaborative		Compromised
Supported		Stunted
Recognized		Ridiculed
Developed		Diminished
Creative		Crushed

KNOW WHERE YOU'RE GOING, HOW TO GET THERE, AND IF YOU'RE IN THE RIGHT VEHICLE

Mile Markers and Dashboards. Simple roadside markers appear mile after mile along many interstates and highways. Despite their generic look and commonality, they serve travelers well to show the way, to demonstrate progress, and to provide direction. First and foremost, they indicate where you are along the highway. If the numbers are going up, you are heading north; if they are going down, you are traveling south. This may not seem like a big deal, but if you have ever traveled in remote areas with which you are unfamiliar, heading in the wrong direction after a quick stop at a service station is not that hard to do. Many mile markers even correspond with exit numbers to help drivers anticipate when their exit is approaching. Even if your destination is many miles away, each passing marker is a clear, evident sign of forward moving progress. Mostly, though, they come in very handy if you find yourself stranded along a desolate road calling for help. A mile marker will serve as a great friend when a person on the other end of the call asks where you are.

Educational goals require the same type of simple markers to guide those pursuing long-range destinations of improvement. Having clear and distinct markers helps everyone know if they are making the necessary progress along the way. They can show us where we're headed, provide indication of our progress, give direction as needed, and even create a sense of accomplishment. Professors and authors, Chip and Dan Heath of *Switch,* tell readers, "we're interested in goals that are closer at hand . . . we want a *destination postcard*—a vivid picture from the near-term future that shows what could be possible" (p. 76).

Consider, a high school with a goal to improve student attendance. Although this is a common goal among many schools, it is a massive undertaking. Once schools dig beyond typical absences due to sickness, a doctor's appointment, or a family emergency, they often find themselves in challenging situations with no easy answer to ensuring a child goes to school. The tough issues schools face aren't on whether an absence is excused or unexcused, but why the student isn't attending, which through some quick investigation often uncovers a myriad of other issues in that student's life. As schools dig into the data, a number of students who don't attend school on a regular basis will surface. A common response is schools deciding to home in on particular groups of at-risk students, but, the harsh reality is conventional methods don't always work. Those working day in and day out with students are fully aware that a repeat ninth grader with two high school credits is definitely at risk and a soon-to-be drop out. Stern warnings, detentions, even a stark reality check of what their future holds may not make the slightest dent. However, schools driven by passion realize there are ways to connect with students, there is hope, and they employ clear strategies to build bridges to students.

On Joe's credenza sits a beautiful clock with the engraving "We did it." He was appreciative when Jamar gave him the clock and he's not sure if Jamar realized how much it meant to him. Not just because it was a thoughtful gift and that Jamar did graduate, although at times they were both uncertain if he would. The clock served as a reminder of time, creating an even greater sense of urgency for Joe, because he knows how time runs out on so many students. Jamar did succeed, he did it, we did it, but like many other students, he had very rocky days academically, with class being the last thing on his mind. Passionate schools are filled with caring educators who know that if the goal is to improve student attendance then relationships built on trust and care are the first step to getting many of our students through the front doors each day.

In any given school, there are pockets of students with severe attendance issues. For many of these learners, school has become more of a reminder for *what they don't know* rather than *what they can learn*. Schools that set goals and live by the mile-marker approach recognize that the goal is the target, but the mile marker creates continuous opportunity checks to ensure progress is being made. Setting a goal like improving attendance by a certain percentage is necessary and often appropriate. But, passionate schools take it one step further. They ensure the goal equates to names and faces that remind them of *the why* behind *the what* that needs to be done. Mile markers can take on a variety of forms, such as the daily check in to see if Jamar was in school, or ensuring an adult mentor touches base to see if he did his homework, or if he even had dinner last night. All are appropriate markers that can be done daily to ensure Jamar is making progress toward his goal. As schools drill down into the core of the attendance issue, setting goals supported by clear markers that demonstrate ongoing progress is the key to success. The mile marker provides insight, stability, and support through very clear targets.

Interestingly, the mile marker doesn't make the work easier, rather it allows for quick checks to see if the intervention strategies are on target. When it comes to attendance, too often schools wait for periodic data reports to determine if they are on track and if student attendance is improving. Unfortunately, too much time passes in between reports, with too many days missed, with too much time gone by and no way to go back. The reality is that poor attendance is common, specific targeted goals are necessary, and when accompanied by markers, there is a greater likelihood of success.

As schools constantly wrestle with improvement goals, such as student attendance, the destination can seem too far away, creating doubt, weariness, and possible notions of defeat. One way to encourage those along the way is using the mile markers for short-term wins. Mile markers create opportunities to recognize success and build positivity into the culture, fueling a commitment to success. The incremental mile markers provide a realistic picture of progress and allow for daily and weekly celebrations. Wins for those intervening on behalf of the students and the students themselves are what sustain the positive momentum and the passion for great work.

Dashboards. In Sir William Osler's 1913 address to Yale students, titled *A Way of Life*, he described his voyage across the Atlantic on an incredible ocean liner and how with a simple push of a button, the ship closed off certain parts, enabling a critical safety feature for water-tight compartments. This was a powerful message at the time, considering the sinking of the Titanic. He urged the students to relate to the ocean vessel and recognize that they also must have the ability to close off compartments that can sink them—compartments in their past and in their future. His method for achieving this was for the students to learn how to live in day-tight compartments.

This sage advice delivered over 100 years ago is still powerful and relevant. As Osler stated, this is "so easy to say, so hard to realize!" (p. 24) because we are always comparing ourselves with the past and looking toward the future, not realizing the power of today. Schools are afflicted by this same mentality. We use the past to set goals for the future, but too often we are uncertain on how to get there and how to move forward. The past is a crippling reminder of poor performance and the future is daunting and overwhelming. So the goal lives on a sheet of paper and not in the hearts of those trying to achieve it. Goals that are broken down into clear activities that are reasonable and serve as quick checks break down the massive effort into realistic compartments. When people know what they need to specifically achieve on any given day, then success is far more likely. Working in day-tight compartments as Osler advises, allow schools to maintain the proper perspective and outlook. It also embodies the spirit of our third mantra mentioned in the introduction—today, there is nothing more important than now!

While the mile marker serves as an indicator of measured progress, the dashboard provides a systems check. A car dashboard allows for a quick assessment on how well the vehicle is operating. Although systems vary and the controls may be more exotic depending on the car, each serve the same basic function—to inform the driver of necessary information to ensure the car is operating smoothly. In education, dashboards serve three primary functions: (1) They provide a basic update designed to help and inform whether or not the interventions and strategies are working. (2) They serve as an opportunity to include the entire team as a one-stop shop where everyone can see the data, report outcomes, and have thoughtful discussions on students. (3) They give those on the frontline a voice. In supported and celebrated environments, those living out the day-to-day plan of action feel a greater sense of community and connection when they have the opportunity to share their ideas and thoughts.

This is where passionate leaders shine. They use the dashboard as an opportunity to make adjustments to the plan, but much of the information is from those doing the grunt work to achieve the goals. This approach not only builds a strong professional community, it deepens everyone's resolve. Think back to our chronically absent students; if the leader realizes early on that the strategies implemented are not working, then based on clear evidence, new ideas suggested from those working directly with the students can be initiated. Not only is this an informed decision, but it also increases communication and an understanding as to why a leader may change course or try new approaches.

Lastly, a by-product of this method is creativity. Developing a routine that checks on the systems in place and whether or not strategies are working allows for greater collaboration when something is not working. This collaboration creates transparency and great teams recognize that collaboration will inspire ideas. This creates a level of transparency, which inspires trust between administrators and teachers, fundamental for passionate schools.

Dashboards represent the details and minutiae associated with many interventions all in the same spot. Schools pursue many worthwhile goals but don't have a basic systems check in place to see if progress is being made. Unfortunately, not every idea, approach, and solution works, but by combining the interventions into one dashboard, with the ongoing, continuous mile-marker mindset, schools can involve a number of people in the discussions that are all focused on the same goal. It's important to note that the dashboard does not need to be sophisticated, but rather informative, consistent, and ongoing.

By embracing the Mile Marker and Dashboard mindset schools are equipped to set clear goals supported by clear measures and a method to check on progress. Passionate schools recognize that the goals worth pursuing are those most difficult to achieve. Yet, that doesn't dissuade them; rather it empowers them. For our chronically absent students, asking them to attend school on a daily basis may seem impossible, unrealistic, and worse yet, not worthwhile. But asking them to attend just the next day is doable. A simple request backed up by ensuring they have an alarm clock, letting them know that you will be there to greet them, and that you are counting on them makes the likelihood of them attending much greater. Care creates connection and connection builds relationships and relationships will be the source ultimately from where goals are achieved. These are the elements necessary for motivation and positive change, the building blocks of passionate schools.

Once this is in place then celebration needs to be incorporated in every possible way. The details of what to celebrate in schools are covered in Chapter 6. As travelers need clear signs to know exactly where they are, so do school staff and students need to know that all of their hard work and progress is appreciated and recognized.

A CULTURE OF CELEBRATION

So at the heart of creating a place where people want to work, feel appreciated, and don't feel alienated or the brunt of criticism is a culture of appreciation and celebration. As Mother Teresa once said, "There is more hunger for love and appreciation in this world than there is for bread." People want to be recognized for efforts and accomplishments and more importantly, they deserve to be, which also creates the necessary connection among staff and their work. Schools don't have to be havens of frustration. It is possible to create an environment where people want to walk through the door, where the energy is palpable, and people feel appreciated and wanted. This is tough to develop for a variety of reasons, but schools that acknowledge the challenges and embrace the passionate mindset learn to ignite the system. The following are two primary ways to develop the passionate mindset in schools:

CREATING A POSITIVE CULTURE BY DESIGN: RECOGNITION AND UNDERSTANDING

1. *Build a culture that **recognizes** achievements.* The truth is not everyone knows how to recognize others. We work in cultures that truly believe that identifying weaknesses rather than celebrating successes is more valuable to overall achievement. However, this widespread belief is being threatened (Hallowell, 2011). This is where the *Mile Marker* is critical. Short-term wins must be identified to help people recognize the progress being made. Not only are short-term wins critical, but we must have a variety of reasons and ways to celebrate. Schools are filled with accomplishments and success stories. Every day, in every school something great happens; we just need to recognize it and appreciate the achievement. Celebration needs to be a mindset, something to look for, anticipate, and seek. Be a celebration hunter! The specifics of what to celebrate is captured in Chapter 6. However, all recognition should be sincere, specific, and timely.

2. *Build a culture that **understands** how to celebrate and show appreciation.* Separating personal and professional celebrations is critical. Honestly, schools are great at throwing parties. However, there is a clear distinction between a party and a celebration. Parties are focused on nonschool-related events: birthdays, weddings, the birth of a child, retirements, and so on. We're not suggesting that you can't throw a party, but real passion and commitment to work is developed when people are connected to what they do and what they are trying to achieve. Passion goes beyond happiness and creates an authentic sense of meaning and reward (Gordon, 2011). Although far different from schools, we can learn how to "treat" employees by looking toward some innovative businesses. VMware, nestled in Palo Alto, stands out for their unique approach to putting their employees first in a profit driven industry. Whether it is their class on "mindfulness for techies" or their belief around "harnessing the power of human difference" through their diversity and inclusion

program (2017), VMware puts employees first (Fortune, 2016). School cultures that understand the needs of their employees and are able to blend both the technical needs of the employee with their overall well-being will achieve greater success.

Although it may be easier to recognize shortfalls and failures and some simply don't want to recognize others or the overall progress, cultures can shift. Whether it's outside forces, like Sean, the cynic believing our schools will never be good enough, or inside voices such as Don—we've already done this, so I'm checking out—or Wanda, who believes there is no way this is going to work, successful systems push forward regardless. They create environments where teachers are believed to be heroes and students are capable of learning and growing.

A Framework for Growth Through Reflection

Think: What Did I Learn?

Plan: What Do I Need to Do?

Act: What Will I Begin Today?

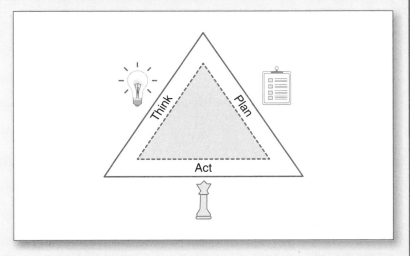

(Continued)

(Continued)

- Refer to Figure 5.1, The Difference Between a Culture of Celebration and Culture of Neglect. Is your current organizational culture one that celebrates and recognizes achievement often and systematically or one where people are mostly neglected and ignored, and what are some of the reasons as to why that may be? *Think*
- How will you shift your mindset to embrace the concept of mile markers and dashboards to recognize success for short- and long-term wins? *Plan*
- What initial action steps do you need to take to design a positive work environment for yourself and others? *Action*

  o Identify your *greatest challenge* regarding the development of a culture that recognizes success and achievement.
  o Identify your *greatest opportunities* regarding the development of a culture that recognizes success and achievement.
  o Identify your *greatest challenge* regarding the development of a culture that systematizes authentic celebration.
  o Identify your *greatest opportunities* regarding the development of a culture that systematizes authentic celebration.

Positive
Educators Ignite
the System

"How management chooses to treat its people impacts everything—for better or for worse."

—Simon Sinek

CELEBRATE LIKE YOU MEAN IT

Simply put, celebrations should be positive, and they should connect people to one another and their work. We divide "celebrating like you mean it" into two equal categories: (1) Infusing positivity at the core of our value systems, *and* (2) Making connections between the people who matter most for our success as an organization. Celebrations in schools have to be genuine, so real that whatever is being presented for celebration is likely going to bring about tears of joy or explosive applause for meaningful work. When we say "celebrate like you mean it," we refer to the celebration itself and the meaning that the celebration provides as an example of the work that people are doing in schools.

Being positive has to be a core value if our schools are going to sustain passion. There's scientific evidence that a positive culture has numerous benefits for employee engagement, including increased productivity and sustainable energy (Seppälä & Cameron, 2015). We boil passion down to making continuous improvements, good-old-fashioned hard work, and being positive, but that can't happen in a culture that zaps energy or where stress is leading to illness and injury. Celebrations, when done authentically, are just the right ingredient to optimize positivity. Tony Schwartz (2012), CEO of The Energy Project, notes that,

> Feeling genuinely appreciated lifts people up. At the most basic level, it makes us feel safe, which is what frees us to do our best work. It's also energizing. When our value feels at risk, as it so often does, that worry becomes preoccupying, which drains and diverts our energy from creating value.

Celebrating people as the leader is not optional if you want a positive work culture and the energy that comes with it. Celebrations are also contagious. The more we celebrate, the more we look for things to celebrate. Because celebrations are positive and uplifting, people naturally look for ways to do so but only when it's a supported practice and recognized as a cultural norm. That's why it's critical to name "positivity" as a core value and celebrations as the practice that leads to sustaining a positive outlook in schools.

Celebrations connect people and act as a reward for doing what matters most to our success together. In *Everyday Courage for School Leaders*, Cathy Lassiter tells readers that celebrations and simple recognition programs can build collective efficacy, the psychological construct that supports our work together as meaningful and effective. Leaders must make the explicit connection between adult actions and meaningful outcomes tied to the goals of the school. When these connections are made, teams and teachers can see that their collaborative efforts are leading to success. Celebrations that connect people to one another and the powerful outcomes of their work inspire positivity and the result of that is passion for the work we do together.

So, celebrate like you mean it. Pick the most important times when people come together to do something that recognizes people and their contributions and be sure that the contributions, large or small, are tied to the most important work that the people in our schools are doing. Later in this chapter, we discuss how to systematize celebrations without them becoming monotonous routines, and we demonstrate the power of diversifying what, why, and who we celebrate.

The ultimate goal for celebrating is that it lifts people and creates a positive energy in the school. That positivity can be carried through the halls and into the classrooms to support students. Positivity is an essential ingredient in passion, and it's something that the leader can create for a school. If you've ever been in a school that seems to have an energetic uplifting vibe, it's the leader who instilled that through celebrations to create a positive atmosphere. With all of the complexities of educating young people, it's critical that the culture is one of passion to include the power of positivity as a characteristic of everyone within the culture. We recognize that this is very complex work, but we don't need to make any more complicated than it needs to be. In fact, we outline what great leaders do to ensure a passionate culture through positivity in the remaining sections of this chapter, and we have found for ourselves that it is quite simple.

TWO DATA TREASURE TROVES: CREATE SHORT-TERM WINS THROUGH GOAL-SETTING

Blanchard and Bowles's (1998) fictitious character, Andy, faced the challenges of a failing corporation around him but overcame adversity as the leader of his department. As the parable unfolds, readers understand that one of the cornerstones to the positive environment that Andy builds is in the recognition of his people as they accomplish their shared goals. For Andy, it was ensuring that the work is worthwhile, setting appropriate markers to determine success, and cheering people along the way. Blanchard and Bowles call that being "gung ho!"

The take-away, though, in terms of creating a positive environment as a factor of passion in schools is that leaders need to set very clear goals and determine with specificity the short-term check-points. As discussed in the last chapter, too often the mile markers of success for a school are test scores, which are not realized until the school year is over and can even have reporting delays into the following school year. This is why test scores cannot be the only indication of success for a school, not because student assessment data is inappropriate as a measurement, but because these scores don't typically allow for celebration in the interim. This is why goal-setting in schools is a critical function of a positive culture and where short-term wins are so incredibly important to sustaining positivity. An exercise in setting achievement goals that aren't tied to test scores is the first step to realizing that shorter-term goals are really important to measuring and celebrating the process of teaching and learning and not just the outcomes.

Your school leadership team can easily do a brain-dump activity regarding all of the data that will work as guideposts for celebrations of successes along the way. But let's consider two important areas where your school can make a difference and measure effectiveness in short-term cycles—teacher-reported grades and student engagement *with* school.

Teacher Reported Grades. One of the untapped treasure troves of school improvement data is the controversial bank of teacher reported grades. From Guskey's (2014) work on grading policies to Shiel's (2017) work on designing better tasks, we somehow can't get grading right, but a good place to start the conversation is by setting goals based on your current student outcome data that teachers are reporting. Because grading is both a place that needs work and a place to develop short-term goals, it's a real win-win in terms of professionally developing teachers to enhance their understanding of grading practices *and* a way to celebrate something that's really important. Grade reporting often occurs in three or four cycles within a school year, and sometimes we define the halfway point with an interim. That's at least three celebrations, with up to eight, depending on your reporting schedule.

The goal with grades is always for the numeric mark or letter grade to represent student learning toward a continuum of mastery (Gentile & Lalley, 2003). This means that we should be working to reduce the number of students earning Ds or Fs. When we've disag-gregated this type of data in schools, at all levels, we've found percent-ages of Ds and Fs that schools were not proud to report and, at times, unaware of. Additionally, the data often tell a much different story about special education students and students of color than what it says about regular education students and their white peers. For these reasons, digging into the data and setting goals is critical for teachers and the school as a community to identify clear areas of need and to set clear targets that need to be met and ultimately celebrated.

Taking this further, data provide ample opportunity to look for short-term wins that everyone can support. Most schools have sys-tems that are set up so that anyone can earn honor roll or other high honors, designed to reward achievement. For example, honor roll might be all As and Bs while high honors is all As. In a system of this kind, an appropriate goal could be to increase the number of stu-dents on honor roll and high honors and to also have indicators in place for students making recognizable progress. The goal is to create opportunities for recognition at all levels. So, when grade levels, teams, and teachers reach new levels of student achievement, it's time to celebrate. Celebrations *instill* positivity, and consistent cele-brations *sustain* positivity. Hard work that leads to success must be celebrated, and passion-driven success demands celebrations by the whole community.

The key is that mile-marker celebrations are embedded in the culture to demonstrate student and staff success outside of the typi-cal ways we recognize achievement. Dr. Matthew Ohlson, from the University of North Florida, relayed a great story to us about how Wadsworth Elementary School is using "mile markers" to celebrate staff and students. Dr. Ohlson works with rural schools in Florida, and elsewhere, to identify "leading (not lagging) indicators of suc-cess. Lagging indicators are data points, such as test scores, while leading indicators include data points around attendance and other measurements." Under principal Dr. Anna Crawford's leadership, Wadsworth is celebrating high attendance rates for students and staff. The school has a Champion Attendance platform that honors the students who attend school every day. The recognition builds excitement and high expectations. This focus and effort to celebrate brought attendance rates up to 96 percent in the time period reported to us. Principal Crawford looks at attendance rates in seven-day increments to be able to dive deeper into reasons why students are absent and to identify and celebrate early wins. We can't teach students if they aren't in school, and attendance is a simple data point that provides tremendous opportunity to celebrate wins and to uncover potentially at-risk students regardless of the locale—rural, suburban, or urban. Dr. Spoor is another leader, in an urban high school, who put together a system to celebrate attendance, and more, for short-term wins.

As we've said, all of stories in this book are real, and we even use real names. We want to introduce you to Dr. Stan Spoor, the former principal of Howard High School of Technology in Wilmington, Delaware. Howard High is a historic school, serving at one time as the only high school for African American students in the state of Delaware. The school, where Martin Luther King Jr. once spoke, is now a nationally recognized vocational technical school nestled in the heart of the city. Dr. Spoor came to Howard at a time when the school was experiencing high teacher turnover, low student perfor-mance, and a need for a strong vision to set a new course. What you'll read here is not the full scope of Spoor's work, which could be a book by itself, but it does demonstrate the power of the early win, the mile marker, and what it takes to celebrate kids and the successes of everyone supporting them.

Actualizing the Power of Data Systems, Short Wins, and Celebrations

Dr. Stanley Spoor, Principal
Howard High School of Technology
Wilmington, Delaware

Stan Spoor was an assistant principal at Howard High School when the team implemented the Triple Crown. It all started, as most initia-tives do, when the data made it clear to the counselors, teachers, and administrative team that too many "really good" kids weren't getting recognized for their efforts and accomplishments in school. Sure, the school, like most, was recognizing kids who had top GPAs, who made all As or Bs, but there was another large segment of students, they concluded it was at least a tenth of the population, who were doing well but without notice.

Stan says that students who do "great" in school inevitably get celebrated. His quandary was about students who might not do "great" things but who surely do "good" enough that we shouldn't let their accomplishments go uncelebrated. The team sat down to discuss and the driving question was "What do kids have to do to show us that they're committed but maybe not superstars?"

The team developed a criteria for the new Triple Crown, which was a 3.0 GPA, 0 or 1 absence, and no discipline record. Several aspects of this were very important to the team. First, they would celebrate Triple Crown earners by the marking period, which made the celebrations a short-term win for the school and for students. This is something that the team wanted because high schools generally celebrate achievement on an annual basis. Second, the GPA calculation is not cumulative. It's only based on one marking period's worth of data, which brings about the third aspect that the team wanted, which is that students get a fresh start at the beginning of each new marking period.

The team was proud of the new initiative because it meant fresh starts and celebrations. A student could do poorly in marking Period 1, missing school often and getting into trouble, but then bounce back during marking Period 2. It means that the adults can act as mentors with the anticipation that students need when they are reinvigorated about school and doing well. And, it also meant that you don't have to be a student with the capabilities of earning all As to get recognized.

The program is layered with celebrations and rewards as well. Students receive a certificate that is sent home. They get their names in the bulletin, listed around the school, and each teacher gets the list to celebrate in unique ways per classroom. The biggest celebrations happen in "shop class" and during the Triple Crown ice cream or pizza party that the school plans each marking period.

A by-product of the program is that staff members and students are tracking data to support the Triple Crown throughout the marking period. As the principal of the school, Stan, recalls the granular aspects of running the program and smiles as he signs the certificates that cross his desk. He tells stories of kids who introduce themselves as Triple Crown earners and how local colleges and universities know the

(Continued)

(Continued)

program from applications to resumes that get submitted for admittance. It's all about finding ways to support more students, celebrate short-term wins in a system that's not set up for it, and infusing positivity into school by leading with passion.

This story demonstrates the power of data systems coupled with the notion of short wins using mile markers. It's only when the whole community comes together through positive celebrations that the ripple effect takes hold, spreading the good work that schools do and creating momentum for the future. Let's take a look at another treasure trove for goals we can celebrate often.

4 Key Takeaways From Dr. Stanley Spoor

1. *Start something new.* Stan knew that he needed a unique way to celebrate students. In his interview with us, he acknowledged that he quickly realized that only the highest performing students were getting recognized. He knew that the masses were being ignored with many achievements not being mentioned, a lot of little wins going unrecognized, and mostly how the "normal" recognition system was limited, failing to motivate an entire student body. He pulled together a group of people, presented a vision for the need to celebrate in a new way, and the Triple Crown was born. Don't be afraid to introduce the need for something new.

2. *Make it formative.* The two best aspects of the Triple Crown are (1) The celebrations happen more often than what we typically see celebrated in high schools. (2) The data used for celebrating get a "restart button" at every marker. This means that we're celebrating with frequency, and we're allowing students to put the past behind them. Celebrations tend to be infrequent and based on cumulative data. The key takeaway here is that you can overcome this problem by making the celebration formative in nature.

3. *Add layers.* The layers of support that the Triple Crown winners get is one of the keys to it being a lasting great initiative. One-and-done award ceremonies don't lift spirits for more than the

time we spend together in the cafeteria or auditorium. The layered recognition, introduced by the plan for Triple Crown, means that the positive infusion moves well beyond the actual award. When considering data usage for celebrating students, be sure to add multiple layers for communicating and recognizing your winners.

4. *Give it a name.* We love the name *Triple Crown.* It's unique, and it stands out. For Stan's school, it even went beyond the school walls as recognizable to community members and local colleges. Naming your award is important to the recipients and the prestige it will get from others.

Student Engagement With School. A second treasure trove of data for short-term meaningful goal-setting is in looking at student engagement with school. We distinguish the difference between student engagement *with* school and engagement *in* school by simply separating what it means to be connected to school outside of the classroom (sports, activities, clubs, etc.), as in *with school*, and active engagement inside the classroom (participation, meeting deadlines, cooperating with peers, etc.), as in *in school*. The research is clear that when students are connected to school in ways that go beyond academics, they do better socially, emotionally, and academically. But, are you tracking that data and setting goals accordingly?

Most schools have offerings that go beyond the school day and even after school buses to support students staying for activities. With that said, we have found that many of the clubs are dominated by students who otherwise would be doing well in school. We have also found that when students who don't typically do well in school participate, they do much better during the times when they are connected. This has been demonstrated in both the evidence we have as school leaders and the research that has been conducted in this area. The reasons for this are endless, but three simple notions surface as to why this kind of effort is so critical for schools:

1. For kids of all ages, the time between the end of the school day and when their parents can re-engage with them can be

dangerous. This "danger zone" can range from anything between idle wasted time that could be spent on something productive to playing video games to using drugs. When kids spend their afternoon in school, engaged in a club, their time is much more productive and they are more protected.

2. When students are connected with school in a way that is not simply core subject matter, they build relationships with teachers and students, often teachers and students who they wouldn't otherwise have contact with, and these relationships support a feeling of belonging, safety, and security in school. In other words, connected students build a sense of community between themselves and the school that makes the school feel more welcome on a regular basis, and they perform better as a result.

3. There's a simple fact that many of the after school activities that schools offer are attractive to kids, and there are explicit and implicit accountability measures for participation. These measures teach kids to behave in ways that they might not exhibit without the connection.

We heard from Bobby McCutcheon, principal at Randall Elementary School in Independence, Missouri. He and his team are serving a highly diverse student population with over 80 percent receiving free-or-reduced lunch. Randall Elementary draws a number of its students from the largest subsidized housing complex in the Midwest. Bobby knows the power of after school programming to support students' needs so the school sets goals around this; they develop new programs, and they celebrate the students who are participating by holding parent nights and assemblies to honor them. He told us about their Genius Hour Club that meets after school. One of the projects that resulted from the club was a student who partnered with the local police department to learn about police dogs. The student interviewed officers and then led a schoolwide assembly with K-9 demonstrations. The student was also able to attend official police dog training sessions, and the department awarded him an official police badge. The school is tracking and increasing the number of students participating, which allows them to celebrate in ways that they didn't dream possible in the past, like attending a student-driven assembly and the wonders that occur when everyone contributes in the ways we discussed in Chapters 3 and 4. Bobby's goal is to get more students involved, and we celebrate the passion at Randall Elementary School.

Clubs like Genius Hour occur when we unleash the power of short-term wins. We have to take small steps, like starting new programs, before big things can happen, like partnerships and school-wide assemblies with dog demonstrations. The first step in short-term goal-setting regarding increasing student engagement with school is to take an inventory of all of the offerings available in your school. What clubs, activities, sports, for example, are offered and during what times of the year? Are there points in the year where offerings are strong and other times when there are only a few selections? How diverse are the offerings in terms of what kids might like to do after school? The second step is in tracking the number of students participating in each of the activities, linking both the number of students to each activity and the individual students participating. There are two final questions to consider: (1) How might you increase the total number of students participating in activities and in each activity? (2) How can you begin to examine student participation on an individual level? Let's consider Everett Meredith Middle School as real example of bringing this work to life.

When T.J. was the principal of Meredith Middle School, the school went from being under review by the state to a top-ten middle school by all accounts. It was truly a team effort, and when T.J. left to pursue a role in the central office of the same district, he couldn't imagine a better replacement than his assistant at Meredith, Nick Hoover.

Nick was ready. His passion for kids and for school success is palpable, and he knew exactly what to do when he took over. For years, the school focused on bolstering after school activities, but Nick had a vision for taking that to another level. With a background in student support services, including time as a dean, a degree in counseling, and a previous role as assistant at Meredith, Nick didn't wait one day on the job before he gathered his team to create the plan and set the new goals.

Tracking Extracurriculars to Engage Students With School and to Celebrate Success

Nick Hoover, Principal
Appoquinimink School District
Middletown, Delaware

When Nick Hoover took over as principal of Everett Meredith Middle School, he had a vision that 100 percent of the student population would be connected to school in a meaningful way outside of their academic experiences. Nick was once a dean of students and with tons of experience as a school disciplinarian; he knew the power of getting kids to participate with school to mitigate poor choices, especially in the middle school years. He also knew that his vision couldn't become a reality without a whole-school effort so he called a summer meeting before the school year started.

Nick's first step was to engage his counselors and student support team in his vision. For three years as an assistant principal in the same school, the team had made serious efforts to engage students in extracurriculars, but they needed a new push. He sat with the team and asked questions about how many offerings they had, how they could get more kids engaged, and what it might mean for students and families if they could pull it off. He left them with more questions than answers, and the team came back together in the next week.

The support team was inspired by the vision. By the time they came back together, the counselors had assembled a pamphlet that outlined all of the offerings and what students did in each of the activities. They presented it as an advertisement strategy as well as parent information. Each student would get a pamphlet four times a year as the new activities corresponded with their marking periods.

The second document that the counselors had created was a Google Sheet for the whole school to use collectively. It was organized by activity and it listed every single student in the school. The goal was to track who was participating in which activities, how many students per activity, and who wasn't participating at all. Nick was thoroughly impressed with his team, and he asked them to present the new vision at the opening staff meeting for the year.

At the staff meeting, the excitement was high and everyone could feel the positivity in the room. Nick praised the support team and the staff cheered at the new goal. Teachers and support staff were excited to see more students participating, and they had such great passion for the extracurricular activities that they each sponsored. In fact, after the meeting, several staff members approached Nick with new ideas for after school activities that they thought would work—a strategic gaming club, a scrapbooking club, and a running group. One new club, run by Eddie Chavis, a behavioral interventionist, and Stephen Wilson, a social studies and ELA teacher, is called Meredith Men, which focuses on what it means to be a gentleman. They even wear bowties on Tuesdays.

That year, the tracking system worked better than ever. They set goals using the baseline that had been established the previous year whereby about one-third of the student body was participating. In years past, they tracked the total number of participants but they now had a stronger plan to track by club and by student demographics. They even developed a spreadsheet that showed every student and the activities joined by marking period to see who was participating and how often. Ultimately, they celebrated both the tracking system and the participation numbers at each of the four quarters. It energized the staff to see the numbers grow, and that passion recycled itself back into more activities and greater participation.

That first year, the team set a goal of half the students participating and they met it. They took one-third to one-half in one year. The celebrations at each quarter were met with cheers, and tons of parents commented on how much fun their kids were having in the after-school offerings.

Because they had the data on the individual students who didn't participate, it was easy to entice new students at the turn of every quarter. The big push was to culturize engagement by ensuring that every incoming sixth grader was involved. More staff were involved than ever before, and it made a positive impact on the school.

Nick was impressed with his staff and their efforts, but it didn't stop there. The following year they reached two-thirds of the student body participating and they continue year after year, working toward 100 percent. The goal provides meaningful work, short-term wins, celebrations, and a positive outlook for the school community. That's passion in schools at its finest.

Meredith Middle School is a real middle school, and Nick Hoover is an excellent principal, still in his role as we accounted for his success

(Continued)

(Continued)

during the writing of this book. He knows the power of celebrations, the need for short-term wins, and the absolute role that a leader plays in ensuring that positivity is the spark for passion. Celebrating is so critical to positivity in schools that it has to be systematized for the cultural benefits to reach every student and staff member.

4 Key Takeaways From Principal Nick Hoover

1. *Be an advertiser.* Once Nick's team took an inventory of all of their program offerings, they created a catchy and meaningful advertisement for students and families. Doing an inventory is a clear first step. Knowing how many programs you have, what their names are, when they run during the year, and making a list of them will improve participation by itself. Creating a colorful advertisement is even better. The takeaway is that it's important to inform families about all of the after-school activities that are available, even doing a little enticement along the way.

2. *Let creativity flow.* The more creative the program, the more likely it is to generate interest from students who don't typically stay after school. By bringing new and unique offerings to the table, you have a much better chance of attracting *all* students. When a staff member says they want to do a scrapbook club, make it happen.

3. *Improve your tracking system.* One of the keys to getting more and more students involved in nonacademic programs is to have a clear tracking system. Nick's team relentlessly tracked the students each year, using various programs and methods, designed to identify any student who was not involved. You need a strong data-tracking system if you're going to glean the information you need to make change.

4. *Set clear goals.* Once your tracking system is in play, you can see how many students are staying each marking period, halfway through the year, and then annually. Use that information to set clear and realistic goals, moving toward 100 percent participation. It's not enough to say that "we're going to increase participation." You need clear targets.

SYSTEMATIZING CELEBRATIONS

Celebrations have to be part of the culture in schools to reap the benefits of positive passionate people with a common goal. As we've discussed so far, much of a typical school's celebrations are more aligned to parties, such as birthdays and baby showers, which are both important, but not enough to ignite passion through positivity. Schools must have systematic ways in which celebrations are embedded and embraced.

Monthly staff meetings are a place to start, and a way to define the culture of meeting together as a large group for a specific purpose. We call for staff meetings to be broken into thirds: one-third celebration, one-third information, and one-third professional development. The formula must be followed and not deviated from for it to be systematic. This provides both the familiar routine that people like and a way to ensure that our time together is productive since it's often limited.

Once faculty meetings follow this formula, it's important to develop semiformulas within the thirds. For celebrations, this means picking a way to celebrate where everyone can be included in lifting others. A portion of this should be the school leaders celebrating the work of the staff, individuals and teams, as well as a way for staff members to celebrate one another. We end this segment with a short list of three ways in which this might occur within the one-third celebration portion of your meeting, and we dive into the next segment of this chapter with *what* and *why* you might celebrate in your school to improve positivity.

- *Principal Passion Prizes*—prizes given by the principal to two people whose work exemplified the vision and mission of the school in the past month. We'll say more about budgeting for "prizes" at the end of this chapter.
- *Peer Recognition Certificates*—each month, five staff members recognize one peer for outstanding work in the past month. The next month, the five who were recognized have the responsibility to do the same for a peer.
- *Difference Makers Award*—team, department, or grade-level leaders recognize peers through their classroom visits, identifying one person per department who is demonstrating outstanding instructional practices in the classroom.

DEFINING *WHAT* AND *WHY* WE CELEBRATE

Celebrations that are meaningful reward people for more than just achievement. It's important to define upfront what you plan to recognize within the culture and why we recognize certain behaviors. We have five reasons to recognize people in schools that fall into two categories: effort and excellence. Notice, though, that only one of the five celebrates excellence. This is because excellence should be a true achievement for only mastery, something that only your most highly effective educators demonstrate on a regular basis, and we want to instill a culture where effort, including growth, energy, innovation, and risk-taking are supported as a norm.

The first area to look for to celebrate is in the places where *growth* is evident. This is the mindset that we want our educators to have and to instill in students so we have to support it with celebrations. This is our first area of effort. This might be a new teacher, making strides toward excellence, but where improvements have been identified and then realized. It might as well be an experienced teacher who is also realizing growth in an area, trying something that isn't necessarily innovative but that's nonetheless new to her after a recent professional development experience. *Example*: You have a new teacher who needs to tighten up classroom management. She demonstrates a few new strategies in a recent walkthrough. You celebrate both the growth and the mindset she has with a *Principal Passion Prize for Making Growth With Student Engagement*.

The second area to look for to celebrate is in places where you find *extreme work ethic* and energy toward a school or personal goal. This is different than growth, and could include growth, but it's a place where you're finding an above-and-beyond level of energy. This is the second area of effort in the five areas to celebrate. *Example*: An interventionist or dean is going above and beyond in the morning for bus duty and again in the afternoon. He is the first one to arrive and the last one to leave, standing in the cold, rain, or snow with consistent energy to ensure that all kids are safe as they enter the building. A peer on the student support team celebrates this energy with a *Peer Recognition Certificate for Energy and Enthusiasm in Supporting Student Safety*.

The third area to look for to celebrate is in places where you find educators doing something altogether new, *taking risks*, and innovating for the success of students. School leaders have to support innovation or status quo will be the norm rather than taking a risk with something new. This is the third area to celebrate in the effort category, specifically because the innovative practice might not be excellent, but the effort in trying something new is worth celebrating to build the culture of innovation and risk-taking needed to push the school forward. *Example*: A midcareer teacher has done some research on a few apps, participated in a Twitter chat or two to learn more about how to use the technology, and then implements something using her 1:1 technology that no one else in the school has yet to discover. You see this during a walkthrough and ask her to present at a faculty meeting where you follow her presentation with a celebration, giving her a *Principal Passion Prize for Innovation in the Classroom*.

The fourth and last area of effort to look for to celebrate is the places where we find our unsung heroes, people doing the *small things*, making minor lifts, but constantly adding value. We celebrate the small things that matter because it's the efforts of everyone that make up the team. It's why soccer commentators make just as big a deal out of the pass as they do the goal. *Example*: One of the department members in the English department keeps team meeting and PLC notes for every meeting during the year. Her notes are detailed and distributed following the meeting and they drive the agenda of the following meeting. The team has recognized this as a pillar of their success with student achievement. The department chair recognizes her with a *Difference Maker Award for Keeping the Meetings on Track With a Small Lift With Big Value Award* at the faculty meeting.

The final and fifth area for celebration is for staff who *display excellence* in their roles in one way or another. This is for mastery and reserved for the highest standards. We celebrate excellence to recognize those who have skills that many of us will never develop, to support what we want to reach for, and to show others what excellence really looks like. Excellence is often defined in our evaluation rubrics but is too often handed out too freely for it to be meaningful. We keep this area of celebration limited to maybe one or two people per month in the third of our faculty meeting that we use for celebrations, giving out this award less than twenty times each school year. *Example*: During peer walkthroughs, a one teacher observes her peer demonstrating mastery with a Kagan structure. They both have been trained so she knows that it's genuinely perfect in its execution. This teacher is known for excellence with collaborative structures but hasn't been celebrated publicly for it outside the professional development he has done in small groups and at PLCs. She celebrates the excellence with a *Peer Recognition Certificate for Excellence With Student Collaboration* at the next faculty meeting, and the staff cheers with joy at the value that is being added to the whole school.

Note that in each case the awards are specific with names for their purpose and the award itself is named for the specific effort or excellence behavior that was observed. Naming practices brings them to life and embeds them in the culture rather than any random awards for randomly selected behaviors. In their work *Practice Perfect*, Lemov, Woolway, and Yezzi (2012) identify this practice of naming as

Figure 6.1 Celebration Model

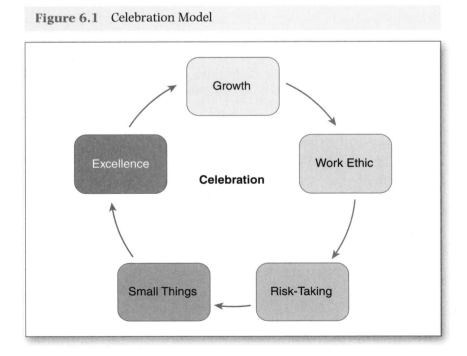

something to do in the classroom to develop routines, and we're using it in faculty meetings to do the same and to model what we want teachers to do in the classroom. That doesn't mean that peer and department-chair awards won't sometimes deviate, but doing so will have a far better chance of systematizing the celebrations, keeping the positive momentum and sustaining passion over time.

DIVERSIFYING THE *WHO*

Great school leaders recognize that the school is made up of more than just the front lines. We've made the argument that teachers aren't celebrated the way they should be, but the sentiment becomes twofold for counselors, nurses, educational diagnosticians, psychologists, secretaries, custodians, nutrition workers, volunteers, and everyone who makes up the Total School Community (TSC). No matter what list we try to assemble, we'll miss someone who works in your school, but the point is that you should know who these people are and how they contribute to the overall culture that makes your school a great place. A great example of this is the *Harvard Heroes Program* (2017), which recognizes a vast array of exceptional staff who exemplify the mission of Harvard.

TECHNICAL TIP #1: BUILDING THE BUDGET TO CELEBRATE

It's generally a School Budget 101 discussion that using school funds to purchase party materials, gift cards, T-shirts, flowers, or anything used for celebration is a big no-no. Principals can get into real trouble if they're using school funds in this way, but there are ways to build internal budgets for celebrations so that your Principal Passion Prize is not a trinket. We outline a few ways below for doing so. It takes some elbow grease but it's worth having food and fun during meetings and events.

1. *Ask for financial donations.* There are often community organizations, restaurants, and businesses that are looking for ways

to put together philanthropic efforts. Think first about the organizations that the school already supports so that it's a partnership and not just an ask. We've used technology companies, insurance companies, student picture studios, and other establishments so that the agreement is reciprocal. Without mixing dollars, develop a special internal account that holds funds specific to celebrations.

How-To: Take inventory of the companies that you're currently paying for services. Turn that into a two-way street. There are always businesses, both locally and nationally, who are supported by teachers and the teaching profession. You would be surprised by the generous offers from even a local sandwich shop where all of the teachers stop for lunch on PD days. If your efforts are helping them with business and advertisement, kick up the relationship to a new level.

---

2. *Sell, sell, sell.* Schools can make a few hundred dollars a year from vending machines. Snacks and soft drinks are a nice touch to the faculty workroom and they can be lucrative as well. We don't advocate for student fundraisers to ever go toward staff celebrations, but you might have a special philanthropic group like your National Honor Society that would raise a small amount through fundraising with staff celebrations as the designated purpose for the raised funds.

How-To: Make it about leadership. Many of the school's leadership teams are able to raise funds for different organizations. Although we're not big fans of fundraisers because we believe that students should have access without having to pay, we do see a benefit to student leadership groups taking on small projects to raise funds toward special interests. United Way and American Cancer Society, for example, are places to direct students' passion for philanthropy. The internal account for celebrations can be setup for donations from groups who are raising funds and awareness toward important social affairs. Just be sure that the student leaders always know *why* they are raising money and *who* the money supports.

3. *Ask for physical donations.* Any small gifts to go with the certificates and celebratory awards makes them that much more special. Local stores are often willing to donate annual gift cards. If you're doing nine faculty meetings a year and presenting to ten people per time, that's just under a 100 small gifts that you need to gather. Even a $5 gift card for coffee is great, and the local coffee shop wins too because your school will start to develop brand loyalty.

How-To: With physical donations, like gift cards or even a book, don't just ask for the item as a blanket award to be given out. Be specific with *why* and even *who* will end up with the award so that the business owner knows just how their gift is being used. Let them share in the pride by inviting them to give out the award and tell the story about why it's so important to celebrate the people. It's far more likely that they'll be willing to help if they know the rationale behind your request.

The tip here is to build your bank account up to a reasonable amount so that you're never scrounging before a celebration. You don't need a ton of money but food at meetings goes along way, and you can't use taxpayer dollars for that. Celebrate like you mean it and crank up the positivity with the money you raise.

TECHNICAL TIP #2: HIRING POSITIVE PEOPLE

Because positivity is so important to work culture, performance, and passion in schools, it's at the top of the list of characteristics you want in a newly hired teacher. Emma Seppälä, author of *The Happiness Track*, tells *Harvard Business Review* (HBR) readers that when teams work together in a positive manner, they are more productive. So far, we've addressed ways that leaders can inspire passion through creating a positive environment, but it's actually easier if you hire positive people in the first place. There is the simple fact that some people are naturally more positive than others so we're on the lookout for the naturals. Here are three practical ways that you can do your best to include positivity in the hiring process. Of course, hiring practices are flawed for all three of our important passion characteristics—positivity, a desire to grow, and work ethic—but that doesn't mean we can't be strategic about looking for them.

1. *Add it to the job description.* There's no reason that the job posting for teachers shouldn't say: *We're looking for positive people to join us in our mission to meet every student's academic and social needs. We consider positivity to be a key attribute in teachers and negative people should not apply.* We advocate for a very clear job description so that you can attract the key characteristics you're looking for in the candidates. Generic descriptions attract generic people. When you're looking for dynamic passionate people, you have to be deliberate about it.

2. *Ask for examples in the interview.* Ask the interviewee for an example of a time when they overcame their own negative thought or the negative thoughts of others in a situation at work. Listen for examples that demonstrate the ability to remain positive no matter what the situation is or how bad it becomes. There should be a balance of personal leadership and professional humility in the answers you get or the candidate might not be a good fit for your school.

3. *Use a scenario as a test.* Provide a fictitious but believable example and ask how the candidate might respond. Tell a story about a circumstance where two other faculty members were talking negatively about the school, or even a student, over lunch, and leave it open ended to see how the candidate might handle the scenario. At best, you're looking for a person who is willing to confront the negativity and, at a minimum, you're looking for a person to get themselves out of the situation before they're dragged into the discussion.

Again, as with most hiring practices, interviewing has its flaws, but when we're looking for specific characteristics, we have to post for them and double down with questions and scenarios during the hiring process.

A Framework for Growth Through Reflection

Think: What Did I Learn?

Plan: What Do I Need to Do?

Act: What Will I Begin Today?

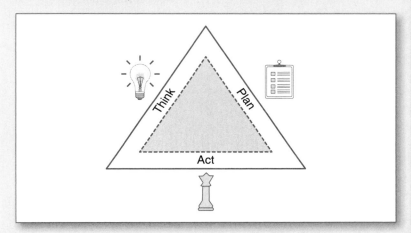

- What is one data point that can be used for short wins and celebrations within your organization? *Think*
- As you plan to develop your system of celebration, what is one area that you can celebrate and recognize today? *Plan*
- What is the first step that you will take to build a community that recognizes and rewards hard work and accomplishments? *Action*

Conclusion

A Blueprint for Sustaining Passion in Our Schools

Passion is an integral aspect of anything worth doing or remembering. We consider passion to be *the* ingredient to ignite desire, fuel efforts, and squelch doubts or fear. Through passion, we fuel our intensity, hope, and care for others along with any and all positive outcomes for our students. Knowing that the ultimate goal of our schools is to educate students to be productive contributing citizens, skilled to accomplish incredible things, our focus as a global community must be on supporting educators and their students. By recognizing that schools are now the new community hubs, the centers of growth and development for more than just our students, our schools need the right resources, recognition, and reinforcement to achieve this monumental task. For this attitude and mindset to grow, it must start among those in the ranks at every level. We must take pride in what we do and the responsibility for the outcomes. We cannot be the ones who trip up our own efforts and trap our own thinking in the process. Passionate educators truly have the possibility to lead a revolution that can change our approach to reform, our view of schools, and our belief in educators and the communities in which they work. It starts with us. We have to quit majoring in the minors, quit praying for a lighter load, and quit telling the world about our problems. We have to start working to get better, start doing things differently, and start celebrating our successes. It starts on the inside (Elmore, 2004), not by changing policy or mandating best practices.

Education is a challenging profession, riddled with obstacles that allow for dissension, confusion, and blame. The development and education of a child is not a simple equation and does not follow a straight and easy path. However, what we do know is that building a culture of learning among educators transforms classrooms and impacts student performance. Creating this culture requires a mindset that acknowledges challenges and works to overcome them, embraces the grind and looks for small and big wins, and admits failure but finds reasons to celebrate. The rewards for a successful student are unparalleled, and we must be willing to forge our efforts with positivity to shift our thinking from *what is* to what *will be*.

We wrote this book as a call to action to inspire the educational community to build relationships, learn from one another, get moving faster, and celebrate louder. We heard from so many leaders in the process that we can't name them all, and the stories are still pouring in via Twitter and other media outlets. We simply asked about passionate leadership, and the people spoke, which is why we vehemently encourage you to grow your network, connect on social media, learn from others, and share your story. The blueprint to sustain passion is clear—we need growth-oriented thinkers, we need an uncompromising work ethic, and we need positivity in our core. That's exactly what the people said when we asked about passion.

We heard from Jessica Torres, education specialist, in Texas, about a professional development bingo she was using to grow her staff. Jenna Magee, a Delaware teacher-leader, told us how she conducted a personality test with teachers to provide reflection time and feedback for growth. Superintendent Anthony Dent from New Jersey told us about a teacher, Brian Meakim, who is gamifying all his activities to improve both rigor and engagement, a unique contribution that we loved. We heard from STEM Club leader Dana Hand who started a club from scratch as a teacher-leader. We got news from Denise Parks, head of schools for a charter school, who said that they were celebrating teachers and their personal interests on Twitter and Facebook to build a sense of community. Beatrice Holmes, from Georgia, highlighted a teacher, Kira Cooper, who is using data notebooks with students to celebrate short-term wins.

Lastly, we heard from Jordan Estock who is working diligently to involve female students in his engineering classes, clubs, and camps. The stories were endless, inspiring, and all connected to growing faster, contributing differently, and celebrating positive outcomes for students.

Our efforts are designed to change schools, districts, and systems. Most importantly, our desire is to change you. Individuals, like you, comprise our system, and for true and lasting change to occur, it will be through the dedication and commitment of people who embrace the call to help students win. To do so, you need to take time to self-reflect and to identify where you are as a passionate educator, where you need to be as a current or future leader, and how you will get there. This book provides a blueprint for how to create the necessary changes in your schools, and among your people, but you must decide if you are willing to take the steps necessary to lead yourself and others to do great things.

Reflection: Culture of Learning

Within the scope of a culture of learning, reflect on how you rate your own desire to learn and improve professionally. Do you take ownership of your own growth and seek out opportunities or do you fall "victim" to the belief that it's someone else's role to professionally develop you? Passionate educators understand the power of identifying their own needs and seeking out ways to improve them through new learning experiences and feedback. Take a moment to reflect on how well you embody a culture of learning. Using a 5-point scale, 1 being ineffective and 5 being highly effective, rate yourself:

My Growth Mindset:

- I actively seek opportunities to improve myself.

  1   2   3   4   5

- I embrace the idea that my growth is my own responsibility.

  1   2   3   4   5

- I yearn for feedback on my practice and commit to making changes based on it.

  1   2   3   4   5

Reflection: Wonder of a Work Ethic

Within the scope of the wonder of a work ethic, rate your commitment to working within the system to ensure that students are given every opportunity to succeed and that you're contributing with your best efforts. Do you work with others to find unique ways to support students? Do encourage students to go beyond their own self-imposed limitations? Do you see yourself as a leader? Passionate educators realize that reaching students is a challenge, but they never give up. Take a moment to reflect on how well you embody the wonder of a work ethic. Using a 5-point scale, 1 being ineffective and 5 being highly effective, rate yourself:

My Work Ethic:

- I actively seek ways to make a difference for all students.

  1   2   3   4   5

- I make uniquely new and different contributions to my school community.

  1   2   3   4   5

- I take on official and unofficial leadership roles in my school community.

  1   2   3   4   5

Reflection: A Culture of Celebration

Within the scope of a culture of celebration, rate your level of personal positivity and commitment to short-term wins. How well do you celebrate yourself and others? Do you find opportunity to enrich others or do you look for reasons to complain? Do you acknowledge and celebrate small and big wins? Do you champion efforts, risk-taking, and excellence? Passionate educators know that the deeper the connection they make with the work the more gratifying and meaningful their efforts will be. Take a moment to reflect on your attitude and how well you celebrate others. Using a 5-point scale, 1 being ineffective and 5 being highly effective, rate yourself:

My Positive Attitude:

- I am a positive force within my school.
  1   2   3   4   5

- I frequently celebrate students and staff based on short-term wins.
  1   2   3   4   5

- I celebrate the connections that students make with school outside of the classroom.
  1   2   3   4   5

Willingly taking a hard look at where you are and where you want to be is challenging. It's the first step in making the necessary changes for the future. We enter so many different endeavors with hope, faith, and passion that often lose their luster and allure. The vibrancy fades and we find ourselves going through the motions wondering what happened. We end this work with the encouraging belief that your reality is what you allow it to be. Decide today to live as a passionate educator, knowing that there is a child right now who needs you to be at your very best. Decide to join us, and the educators we've featured herein, to make a difference by learning to grow faster, contribute in a new way, and celebrate more. Use our three mantras for passionate leadership, and let us know about your story. #passionateleadership

1. *Today* I will grow by challenging myself to be the best I can.

2. *Today* I will work harder than yesterday because there isn't anything more important than now.

3. *Today* I will lift people through positivity.

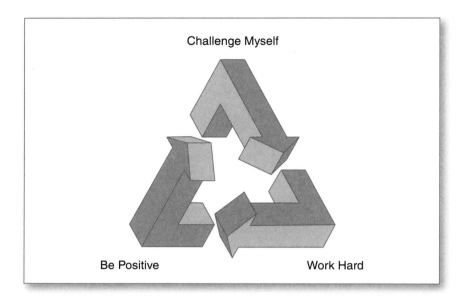

References

Achor, S. (2013). *Before happiness: The 5 hidden keys to achieving success, spreading happiness, and sustaining positive change.* New York, NY: Crown.

Alvy, H. (2017). *Fighting for change in your school: How to avoid fads and focus on substance.* Alexandria, VA: ASCD.

America's Promise Alliance. (2018). *2018 Building a grad nation: Progress and challenge in raising high school graduation rates.* Retrieved from http://gradnation.americaspromise.org/2018-building-grad-nation-report

Ast, H. (2017, December 13). *Calling on business leaders to close the soft skills gap.* Retrieved from https://www.uschamberfoundation.org/blog/post/help-close-soft-skills-gap

Bambrick-Santoyo, P. (2012). *Leverage leadership: A practical guide to building exceptional schools.* San Francisco, CA: Wiley.

Bandura, A. (1994). Self-efficacy. In V. S. Ramachaudran (Ed.), *Encyclopedia of human behavior* (Vol. 4, pp. 71–81). New York: Academic Press.

Bashant, J. (2014, Fall). Developing grit in our students: Why grit is such a desirable trait, and practical strategies for teachers and schools. *Journal for Leadership and Instruction, 13*(2), 14–17.

Behar, H., & Goldstein, J. (2009). *It's not about the coffee: Lessons on putting people first from a life at Starbucks.* New York, NY: Portfolio.

Blanchard, K. H., & Bowles, S. (1998). *Gung ho! Turn people on in any organization.* New York, NY: William Morrow.

Blanchard, K. H., & Johnson, S. (1982). *The one minute manager.* New York, NY: William Morrow.

Blankstein, A., Noguera, P., & Kelly, L. (2015). *Excellence through equity: Five practices of courageous leadership to guide achievement for every student.* Alexandria, VA: ASCD.

Bray, B. A., & McClaskey, K. A. (2017). *How to personalize learning: A practical guide for getting started and going deeper.* Thousand Oaks, CA: Corwin.

Brim, B., & Asplund, J. (2009). *Driving engagement by focusing on strengths.* Retrieved from https://news.gallup.com/businessjournal/124214/driving-engagement-focusing-strengths.aspx

Cable, D. M. (2018). *Alive at work: The neuroscience of helping your people love what they do*. Boston, MA: Harvard Business Review Press.

Carroll, S. R., & Carroll, D. (2000). *Ed Marketing: How smart schools get and keep community support*. Bloomington, IN: National Educational Service.

Carver-Thomas, D., & Darling-Hammond, L. (2017, August 16). *Teacher turnover: Why it matters and what we can do about it*. Retrieved from https://learningpolicyinstitute.org/product/teacher-turnover-report

Clifton, D. O., & Nelson, P. (1992). *Soar with your strengths: A simple yet revolutionary philosophy of business and management*. New York, NY: Dell.

Common Core State Standards. (2018). Retrieved from www.corestandards.org

Compton, R. (Producer). (2008). *2 million minutes* [Motion picture]. United States: 2 Million Minutes.

Cooper-Kahn, J., & Dietzel, L. (2009, February). *Helping children with executive functioning*. Retrieved from https://www.chadd.org/AttentionPDFs/ATTN_02_09_ExecutiveFunctioning.pdf

Council of Chief State School Officers. (2018). *States leading for equity: Promising practices advancing the equity commitments*. Retrieved from https://ccsso.org/sites/default/files/2018-03/States%20Leading%20for%20Equity%20Online_031418.pdf

Duckworth, A. (2016). *Grit: The power of passion and perseverance*. New York, NY: Scribner.

Dweck, C. (2008). *Mindset: The new psychology of success*. New York, NY: Ballantine Books.

Dweck, C. (2015, September 22). *Carol Dweck revisits the "growth mindset."* Retrieved from https://www.edweek.org/ew/articles/2015/09/23/carol-dweck-revisits-the-growth-mindset.html

Dweck, C. (2016, January 13). *What having a "growth mindset" actually means*. Retrieved from https://hbr.org/2016/01/what-having-a-growth-mindset-actually-means

Edmonds, S. C. (2014). *The culture engine: A framework for driving results, inspiring your employees, and transforming your workplace*. Hoboken, NJ: Wiley.

Elmore, R. (2004). *School reform from the inside out: Policy, practice, and performance*. Cambridge, MA: Harvard Education Press.

Epstein, J. L., & Salinas, K. C. (2004, May). *Partnering with families and communities*. Retrieved from http://www.ascd.org/publications/educational-leadership/may04/vol61/num08/Partnering-with-Families-and-Communities.aspx

Epstein, J. L., Sanders, M. G., Simon, B. S., Salinas, K. C., Jansorn, N. R., & Van Voorhis, F. L. (2002). *School, family, and community partnerships: Your handbook for action* (2nd ed.). Thousand Oaks, CA: Corwin.

Erickson, T. (2008, June 5). Do we need titles? *Harvard Business Review.* Retrieved from https://hbr.org/2008/06/do-we-need-titles

Fortune. (2016, March 8). *Human capital 30: Companies that put employees front and center.* Retrieved from http://fortune.com/2016/03/08/human-capital-30/

Fullan, M. (2011a, May). *Learning is the work.* Retrieved from https://docs.google.com/viewerng/viewer?url=http://michaelfullan.ca/wp-content/uploads/2016/06/13396087260.pdf

Fullan, M. (2011b, October). *Whole system reform for innovative teaching and learning.* Retrieved from https://michaelfullan.ca/wp-content/uploads/2016/06/Untitled_Document_5.pdf

Fullan, M. (2014). *The principal: Three keys to maximizing impact.* San Francisco, CA: Wiley.

Fullan, M., & Quinn, J. (2016). *Coherence: The right drivers in action for schools, districts, and systems.* Thousand Oaks, CA: Corwin.

Gallup. (2014). *State of America's schools.* Retrieved from http://www.gallup.com/services/178709/state-america-schools-report.aspx

Gentile, J. R., & Lalley, J. P. (2003). *Standards and mastery learning: Aligning teaching and assessment so all children can learn.* Thousand Oaks, CA: Corwin.

Gordon (2011). *The seed: Finding purpose and happiness in life and work.* Hoboken, NJ:

Gostick, A., & Elton, C. (2009). *The carrot principle: How the best managers use recognition to engage their people, retain talent, and accelerate performance.* New York, NY: Free Press.

Guskey, T. (2014). *On your mark: Challenging the conventions of grading and reporting: A book for K–12 assessment policies and practices.* Bloomington, IN: Solution Tree Press.

Hallowell, E. M. (2011). *Shine: Using brain science to get the best from your people.* Boston, MA: Harvard Business Review Press.

Hargreaves, A., Boyle, A., & Harris, A. (2014). *Uplifting leadership: How organizations, teams, and communities raise performance.* San Francisco, CA: Wiley.

Harvard Heroes Program. (2017). Retrieved from https://hr.harvard.edu/harvard-heroes-program

Hattie, J. (2009). *Visible learning: A synthesis of over 800 meta-analyses relating to achievement.* New York, NY: Routledge.

Heath, C., & Heath, D. (2010). *Switch: How to change things when change is hard.* New York, NY: Broadway Books.

Hoerr, T. R. (2017). *The formative five: Fostering grit, empathy, and other success skills every student needs.* Alexandria, VA: ASCD.

Johnson, W. (2018, May 8). Why talented people don't use their strengths. *Harvard Business Review.* Retrieved from https://hbr.org/2018/05/why-talented-people-dont-use-their-strengths

Joyce, B., & Calhoun, C. (2010). *Models of professional development: A celebration of educators.* Thousand Oaks, CA: Corwin.

Kirsch, V., Bildner, J., & Walker, J. (2016, July 25). Why social ventures need systems thinking. *Harvard Business Review.* Retrieved from https://hbr.org/2016/07/why-social-ventures-need-systems-thinking

Kotter, J. P. (2014). *Accelerate.* Boston, MA: Harvard Business School Press.

Lassiter, C. (2017). *Everyday courage for school leaders.* Thousand Oaks, CA: Corwin.

Lemov, D., Woolway, E., & Yezzi, K. (2012). *Practice perfect: 42 rules for getting better at getting better.* San Francisco, CA: Jossey-Bass.

Lencioni, P. (2002). *The five dysfunctions of a team: A leadership fable.* San Francisco, CA: Jossey-Bass.

Levin, B. B., & Schrum, L. R. (2017). *Every teacher a leader: Developing the needed dispositions, knowledge, and skills for teacher leadership.* Thousand Oaks, CA: Corwin.

Life. (1958, March 24). *Crisis in education: Two pupils? One in the U.S., the other in the U.S.S.R.? Point up a U.S. weakness.* Retrieved from http://www.originallifemagazines.com/LIFE-Magazine-March-24-1958-P2616.aspx

Martone, A., & Sireci, S. G. (2009). Evaluating alignment between curriculum, assessment, and instruction. *Review of Educational Research, 79*(4), 1332–1361.

Marzano, R. (2003). *What works in schools: Translating research into action.* Alexandria, VA: ASCD.

Maxwell, J. (2000). *Failing forward: Turning mistakes into stepping stones for success.* Nashville TN: Thomas Nelson.

Maxwell, J. (2010). *Everyone communicates, few connect: What the most effective people do differently.* Nashville, TN: Thomas Nelson.

McLaughlin, M. (2018). *A brain surgeon's tips for handling stress head-on.* Retrieved from https://www.linkedin.com/pulse/brain-surgeons-tips-handling-stress-head-on-mark-mclaughlin-m-d-

McQuaid, M., & Lawn, E. (2014). *Your strengths blueprint: How to be engaged, energized, and happy at work.* Albert Park, Australia: Michelle McQuaid.

Morgan, A., Lynch, C., & Lynch, S. (2017). *Spark: How to lead yourself and others to greater success.* Boston, MA: Houghton Mifflin Harcourt.

National Center for Education Statistics. (2015). Table 204.75a. *Homeless students enrolled in public elementary and secondary schools, by grade, primary nighttime residence, and selected student characteristics: 2009–10 through 2014–15.* Retrieved from https://nces.ed.gov/programs/digest/d16/tables/dt16_204.75a.asp

National Education Association. (n.d.). *Research spotlight on recruiting & retaining highly qualified teachers.* Retrieved from http://www.nea.org/tools/17054.htm

Nesloney, T., & Welcome, A. (2016). *Kids deserve it: Pushing boundaries and challenging conventional thinking.* San Diego, CA: Dave Burgess Consulting.

Osler, W. (1913), *A way of life: An address to Yale students, Sunday evening, April 20th, 1913.* Retrieved from https://archive.org/details/awayofli feanaddr00osleuoft

Perkins-Gough, D. (2013, September). The significance of grit: A conversation with Angela Lee Duckworth. *Educational Leadership, 71*(1), 14–20. Retrieved from http://www.ascd.org/publications/educa tional-leadership/sept13/vol71/num01/The-Significance-of-Grit@-A-Conversation-with-Angela-Lee-Duckworth.aspx

Protheroe, N. (2009). *Using classroom walkthroughs to improve instruction.* Retrieved from https://www.naesp.org/sites/default/files/resources/2/Principal/2009/M-A_p30.pdf

Rath, T., & Conchie, B. (2009). *Strengths based leadership: Great leaders, teams, and why people follow.* New York, NY: Gallup Press

Ravitch, D. (2010). *The death and life of the great American school system: How testing and choice and undermining education.* New York, NY: Hachette.

Redding, S. (n.d.) *Parents and learning: Educational practices series–2.* Brussels, Belgium: International Academy of Education. Retrieved from http://www.ibe.unesco.org/fileadmin/user_upload/archive/Publications/educationalpracticesseriespdf/prac02e.pdf

Redding, S. (1991). What is a school community, anyway? *The School Community Journal, 1*(2), 7–9. Retrieved from www.adi.org/journal/fw91/Editorial-ReddingFall1991.pdf

Reeves, D. (2009). *Leading change in your school.* Alexandria, VA: ASCD.

Reeves, D. (2016). *From leading to succeeding: The seven elements of effective leadership in education.* Bloomington, IN: Solution Tree Press.

Resnick, L. B., Rothman R., Slattery, J. B., & Vranek, J. L. (2002, May). Benchmarking and alignment of standards and testing. *CSE Technical Report.* Retrieved from https://www.achieve.org/files/TR566.pdf

Rock, D., & Grant, H. (2016, November 4). Why diverse teams are smarter. *Harvard Business Review.* Retrieved from https://hbr.org/2016/11/why-diverse-teams-are-smarter

Rosenthal, R., & Jacobsen, L. (1968). *Pygmalion in the classroom: Teacher expectation and pupils' intellectual development.* New York, NY: Holt, Rinehart & Winston.

Ryan, L. (2016, April 8). The truth about 'performance improvement plans.' *Forbes.* Retrieved from https://www.forbes.com/sites/lizryan/2016/04/08/the-truth-about-performance-improvement-plans/#4a95818a3b36

Scholastic and The Bill & Melinda Gates Foundation. (2011). *Primary sources: America's teachers on America's schools.* Retrieved from http://www.scholastic.com/primarysources/pdfs/100646_ScholasticGates.pdf

Schwartz, T. (2012, January 23). Why appreciation matters so much. *Harvard Business Review.* Retrieved from https://hbr.org/2012/01/why-appreciation-matters-so-mu

Seppälä, E. (2015). Positive teams are more productive. *Harvard Business Review.* Retrieved from https://hbr.org/2015/03/positive-teams-are-more-productive

Seppälä, E. (2017). *The happiness track: How to apply the science of happiness to accelerate your success.* New York, NY: HarperCollins.

Seppälä, E., & Cameron, K. (2015). Proof that positive work cultures are more productive. *Harvard Business Review.* Retrieved from https://hbr.org/2015/12/proof-that-positive-work-cultures-are-more-productive

Shiel, T. (2017). *Designing and using performance tasks: Enhancing student learning and assessment.* Thousand Oaks, CA: Corwin.

Sinek, S. (2011). *Start with why: How great leaders inspire everyone to take action.* New York, NY: Penguin.

Smerek, R. (2018). *Organizational learning & performance: The science and practice of building a learning culture.* New York, NY: Oxford University Press.

Tepper, A., & Flynn, P. (2019). *Feedback to feed forward: 31 strategies to lead learning.* Thousand Oaks, CA: Corwin.

U.S. Chamber of Commerce. (2017). *Calling on business leaders to close the soft skills gap.* Retrieved from https://www.uschamberfoundation.org/blog/post/help-close-soft-skills-gap

University of Pennsylvania. (2018). Penn Resilience Program and PERMA™ Workshops. Retrieved from https://ppc.sas.upenn.edu/services/penn-resilience-training

VMware. (2017, December 08). *Diversity and inclusion.* Retrieved from https://www.vmware.com/company/diversity.html

Whitaker, T. (2012). *What great principals do differently: 18 things that matter most.* New York, NY: Routledge.

Whitaker, T. (2018). *Leading school change: How to overcome resistance, increase buy-in, and accomplish your goals.* New York, NY: Routledge.

Willink, J. (2017). *Extreme ownership: How U.S. Navy SEALs lead and win.* New York, NY: St. Martin's Press.

Wilson, D., & Conyers, M. (2016). *Teaching students to drive their brains: Metacognitive strategies, activities, and lesson ideas.* Alexandria, VA: ASCD.

Index

A SAGE Publishing Company

Helping educators make the greatest impact

CORWIN HAS ONE MISSION: to enhance education through intentional professional learning.

We build long-term relationships with our authors, educators, clients, and associations who partner with us to develop and continuously improve the best evidence-based practices that establish and support lifelong learning.

CORWIN LEADERSHIP

Anthony Kim & Alexis Gonzales-Black
Designed to foster flexibility and continuous innovation, this resource expands cutting-edge management and organizational techniques to empower schools with the agility and responsiveness vital to their new environment.

Jonathan Eckert
Explore the collective and reflective approach to progress, process, and programs that will build conditions that lead to strong leadership and teaching, which will improve student outcomes.

PJ Caposey
Offering a fresh perspective on teacher evaluation, this book guides administrators to transform their school culture and evaluation process to improve teacher practice and, ultimately, student achievement.

Dwight L. Carter & Mark White
Through understanding the past and envisioning the future, the authors use practical exercises and real-life examples to draw the blueprint for adapting schools to the age of hyper-change.

Raymond L. Smith & Julie R. Smith
This solid, sustainable, and laser-sharp focus on instructional leadership strategies for coaching might just be your most impactful investment toward student achievement.

Simon T. Bailey & Marceta F. Reilly
This engaging resource provides a simple, sustainable framework that will help you move your school from mediocrity to brilliance.

Debbie Silver & Dedra Stafford
Equip educators to develop resilient and mindful learners primed for academic growth and personal success.

Peter Gamwell & Jane Daly
Discover a new perspective on how to nurture creativity, innovation, leadership, and engagement.

Leadership That Makes an Impact

Steven Katz, Lisa Ain Dack, & John Malloy
Leverage the oppositional forces of top-down expectations and bottom-up experience to create an intelligent, responsive school.

Peter M. DeWitt
Centered on staff efficacy, these resources present discussion questions, vignettes, strategies, and action steps to improve school climate, leadership collaboration, and student growth.

Eric Sheninger
Harness digital resources to create a new school culture, increase communication and student engagement, facilitate real-time professional growth, and access new opportunities for your school.

Russell J. Quaglia, Kristine Fox, Deborah Young, Michael J. Corso, & Lisa L. Lande
Listen to your school's voice to see how you can increase engagement, involvement, and academic motivation.

Michael Fullan, Joanne Quinn, & Joanne McEachen
Learn the right drivers to mobilize complex, coherent, whole-system change and transform learning for all students.

CORWIN
LEADERSHIP